MLS

$ 11.80

D1400135

A Guidebook
to the Web

A Guidebook to the Web

by
Robert Harris
Vanguard University
(formerly Southern California College)

was conceived by
Joan M. Morris and **Arlen D. Carey**

Dushkin/McGraw-Hill

A Division of The McGraw-Hill Companies

Sluice Dock, Guilford, Connnecticut 06437

Director of Technology: Jonathan Stowe
Developmental Editor II: M. Marcuss Oslander
Design: Lara M. Johnson

—————➤●◄—————

Preface

The explosion of information available today on the World Wide Web has provided instant access to the kind of information that used to be reserved only for those willing to spend hours researching material in journals, newspapers, and specialized books. Now, with the click of a mouse, you are connected not only to this information, but also to the kind of information that may be less than helpful, or worse, intellectually compromising. *WebQuester: A Guidebook to the Web* is designed to help you become a discriminating consumer of information. Beginning with a brief introduction to working with the online supplement to this book, the next chapter gives a basic background to the concept of the World Wide Web, and some critical definitions of terms you will need to operate in the technological world of the Internet. The book then provides comprehensive information on how to conduct searches on the World Wide Web, dealing first with specific tools such as directories and search engines, then with strategies such as multiple-word searches and Boolean Operators. As critical as knowing how to navigate on the Web is the ability to be able to critically assess the quality of material found there. The next chapters give you specific insights into evaluating Web sources, discussing such topics as credibility, accuracy, reasonableness, support, and objectivity, and then provide specific examples of citing Web sources in a paper or a presentation.

Chapters seven and eight discuss the kind of intellectual issues that apply in all areas of discourse: thinking critically, and ethical behavior. How do you test a hypothesis for validity? How can you become aware of logical fallacies in arguments or advertising? How

★ ▼

does your behavior in a computer lab or on a personal Web page affect others who will access your material? How do you know when you're likely to be ripped off? *WebQuester: A Guidebook to the Web* will provide you with some comprehensive answers. The final chapter introduces you to WebQuester, an online supplement that provides Web research exercises to enhance many courses with current content.

Table of Contents

Chapter 1

Working with *WebQuester: A Guidebook to the Web*

Has your mouse run amok? Feel lost in cyberspace? Need to find information fast? This guidebook will give you the kind of help you need to locate really useful information from among the myriad Web sites that exist today on the World Wide Web. Can't decide which sites are worth reading? Which ones contain reliable information? This guidebook will give you the tools you need to critically analyze and assess the material you find. Need to cite the information in a paper or a presentation? This guidebook will also give you the latest techniques for citing Internet materials in your work.

Each chapter focuses on a specific skill that you will need in navigating the World Wide Web. As a practical application of that skill, each chapter has a Web component with several online interactive activities. By working out these activities you will practice and develop the skills discussed in the chapter. This highly effective, unique method of learning is valuable to anyone using the Internet or Web-based materials in class. The skills apply regardless of the specific subject matter you are studying.

The activities that accompany this guidebook are available without charge on the WebQuester site. (See directions below.) No registration is necessary. Simply type the address into your browser and connect.

Please Note:

Other WebQuester titles are available for specific courses. Each one uses this same book and basic exercises, but, in addition, also contains a series of online Web exercises based on carefully selected Web sites that pertain to a specific course. If your instructor decides to use a WebQuester in a particular course, this guidebook is a valuable resource for the kind of exercises that you will do there. If you have already purchased this guidebook, the course-specific WebQuester will be available online for a minimal extra charge. You will need to obtain a registration key and register on the site to use a course-specific WebQuester. For further information about registering for a course-specific WebQuester, see chapter 9.

Accessing the Exercises

In order to access these exercises:

1. Start your Web browser and connect to the Internet.
2. Type in the following Web address (the URL):
   http://www.dushkin.com/webquester/activities/

This will take you to the WebQuester activities Home Page. It should look similar to the one shown in Figure 1 below.

✴ Figure 1 ✴

3. Select the chapter you want to visit.
4. No registration or purchase is necessary to complete the exercises.
5. Read directions carefully. Complete the exercise. Consult the chapter of the book if you need to refresh your memory about procedures. Fill in all blank spaces. Click on "Submit" if indicated. Some of the results may be forwarded to your instructor.

The Activities

Each activity is designed to give you practice in developing the skills discussed in the chapter. For example, in chapter 4, *Search Strategies,* the guidebook discusses several methods you might use in finding information on the Web. The activity that accompanies this chapter asks you to look for information about several businesses by using several methods such as guessing the URL, using *Thunderstone.com,* or *LocalEyes.com.* When you are finished searching, you are asked to provide information about the company and then to fill out a table indicating which method you used and which was most useful. When you submit your response, a graph will show you which method worked best for all students in your class.

In some chapters the activity will direct you to a specific Web site and then ask you to answer some multiple-choice questions about the site. This format will appear in a split screen on your computer with the Web site appearing in the bottom half and the questions in the top half. (See Figure 4 on page 138.) This kind of activity provides you the opportunity to learn to assess the reliability and validity of a number of selected Web sites and to practice finding specific information on them. The activity is identical to the primary kind of activity used in WebQuester.

Web Tip

You may enlarge the top or bottom frame if you prefer to read it on a larger screen. Point your mouse on the dividing line between the frames. When you see two arrows, hold the mouse down and move the line up or down. When you've finished reading the material you can move the line back to its original position.

By completing it here, you will become familiar with the techniques used in working with WebQuester.

Technology is providing new and exciting ways of finding information. As a student you need to know how to best make use of this growing web of knowledge. By reading *WebQuester: A Guidebook to the Web* and completing the activities online you can become Web-savvy and feel comfortable in journeying into cyberspace.

✴ Chapter 2 ✴

The World Wide Web and Web Browsing

Origins of the Web

Where Did the WWW Come From?

If you ever studied Latin prefixes, you might remember that *inter* means *between or among*. And the word *net* is short for *network*. So, literally, the word *internet* means between networks. In other words, the Internet is a collection of computer networks. The idea for the system that developed into the Internet we use today came from the Advanced Research Projects Agency of the U. S. Defense Department. During the cold war of the 1960s, when fear of nuclear war was constant, the government decided to create a computer network that would be completely failsafe—it could continue to operate even if several parts of it were destroyed by an attack. The attack never came, of course, and instead several research universities used the design to link themselves together in the late 1970s and 1980s. By the late 1980s there were several thousand host computers connected together.

The Internet at that time was a text-only medium. A computer or terminal in one city could connect to a host computer in another city and use the host computer's resources (data, processing power, software programs, files). Then, in 1989 a scientist at CERN (a particle physics lab in Geneva) had the idea of creating a graphical user interface for the Web and of allowing data and graphics to be accessed by clicking on a word or title with an embedded address made up of a series of letters or numbers that identified the source— what we now call hyperlinks. Text-only became a thing of the past, as did arcane commands. Using the Internet became easy and intuitive almost overnight. The number of users and the number of Web

✴ **5**

servers exploded. The early growth spurt in the mid-1990s reached 600 percent a year. Today there are millions of servers, tens of millions of users, and hundreds of millions of Web pages.

The original primarily text-based protocols of the Internet still exist, such as Telnet, Gopher, and FTP, but the Web has eclipsed them almost completely. Most online library catalogs that used Telnet, for example, have either already converted to a Web interface or are in the process. And since Web browsers can display Gopher and FTP directories seamlessly, even those older sites that remain appear to be Web-based.

What Does the Web Mean?

Some people lose sight of the meaning of the Web by confusing meaning with technology. The significance of the Web is not about technological breakthroughs any more than the meaning of travel by car is about fuel injectors replacing carburetors. Nor is the excitement about the Web related to its size or that the numbers used to talk about it get bigger every day. The most profound significance of the Web lies in the interconnectedness of people and information. People, businesses, organizations, governments, and information are connected to each other, worldwide, 24-hours a day. Using the Web knowledgeably means having virtually unlimited access to resources and even influencing the rest of the world as never before. Far from isolating people at their computers, the Web has created a global interchange community. If you have ever wondered how a particular news story is reported in New Zealand or the United Kingdom, you no longer have to find a large urban library that subscribes to foreign papers and wait a few days for the current issues to arrive. With a few mouse clicks, you can bring information and viewpoints from foreign countries to your desktop.

How Does the Web Work?

Web Architecture

The Web uses a client-server architecture, which means that everyone using a Web browser is acting as a client (or dependent) computer talking to and making requests of a server (or host) computer. For example, when you sit in a restaurant, you are a client. You tell the waiter what you want and he takes the order to the kitchen where the order is filled. The kitchen is the host or server. The millions of clients and servers are linked together through a network of communications lines (wires, satellites, microwave links, and fiber optic cable) and connection hardware (routers and switches), so that your client can access any host just by typing in the appropriate address.

Web Addresses

Continuing our restaurant analogy further, just as every item on the menu has its own unique name, every document on the Web has its own unique address (known as a URL or Uniform Resource Locator). When you type in a URL or click on a hyperlink (that has the URL embedded in it), your computer sends a request for the document to the address specified. The computer host where the document is stored receives the request and sends the document back to you.

Interestingly, for the sake of efficiency, the document is actually sliced up into pieces, called packets, and each packet is sent along the most available route (by the routers mentioned above) and then reassembled before arriving at your computer. (The Internet is thus called a packet-switching network, because of this method of sending data.) This packet design is a legacy of the Defense Department, which wanted a message to get through even if large parts of the network had been destroyed in a war.

Look at a URL and you can see how addressing works. A URL is divided into sections, like this:

    protocol://servername.domain/path/
        flilename.filetype
    as in
    http://www.sccu.edu/rharris/warning.htm

In the example above, the protocol tells the host computer how to respond to the client. HTTP is hypertext transfer protocol, the set of communication standards used by the Web. Other protocols include FTP, Gopher, SMTP, NNTP, and Telnet.

The server name *www.sccu.edu* is a set of

Web Tip

Note that the Web, because of its origins with certain mainframe computers, uses forward slashes (/) to divide paths, rather than back slashes (\) the way MS-DOS (Microsoft Disk Operating System) paths do. Remember always to use forward slashes when typing in URLs.

letters substituting for a numerical address (in this case, the address 206.215.36.2). Most people find it easier to remember a name than a string of numbers, so the Domain Name System was created to permit this substitution. The domain *edu* indicates an educational institution. The path *rharris* tells the host computer what directory to look in for the file. The path may have several steps in it, depending on how many subdirectories deep the file resides. The file name is the name of the document you have requested, and the file type tells the host (and you) what kind of document is being requested.

Here are a few details about the possible alternatives you will find in these pieces of the URL.

Protocols

HTTP. Hypertext Transfer Protocol controls the vast majority of the Internet now, since it is the protocol of the Web. File names usually end in *.htm* or *.html* (for hypertext markup language), but some newer server software, like that from Microsoft, uses the extension *.asp* (for active server pages). As long as the client and host both know they are using the HTTP protocol, however, the actual file names can be anything.

FTP. File Transfer Protocol is one of the early methods of downloading (retrieving) files from a host computer. It also allows users to upload a file from their computer to the host, so it is still useful. Web page creators can upload their files to their Web servers from anywhere in the world using FTP. The protocol indicator is *ftp://*

Gopher. This is another early protocol, using a menu-based system for choosing files to download. The protocol indicator is *gopher://*

SMTP. Simple Mail Transfer Protocol is the protocol used by many e-mail servers. Newer protocols are now being implemented as well.

NNTP. Network News Transfer Protocol is used by newsgroups for posting and reading messages.

Telnet. This is the protocol used for remotely logging onto a host computer and operating it from your computer as if your

Web Tip

When you type a URL into your browser, you do not need to type in the protocol indicator *http://* because when no protocol is specified, your browser will assume you want HTTP. Try typing in a Web address beginning with the www and watch what happens.

computer were a terminal. Some library online catalogs still use Telnet, though others are converting to a Web interface.

Server Name. The server name chosen usually indicates something about the organization: its name (*www.disney.com*) or main business (*www.chocolate.com*). The server name may have several pieces to it, since a given organization may have several servers (or even several names for the same server). Sometimes you will see pet names for individual servers, just in front of the organization name, as in *darkwing.uoregon.edu,* and other times you will see subdivisions of the main system, as in *www.law.utexas.edu,* or *www.research.digital.com.*

Domain. Each Web site belongs to a top level domain, indicating something about its nature.

The United States uses the following top-level domains:

.edu *Education.*
> These are generally colleges and educational research organizations. Information coming from an educational domain can be from the institution, a faculty member, a student, or a staff member.

.com *Commercial.*
> Businesses of all kinds. These include all businesses from the one-person shop to the corporate giants.

.org *Organization.*
> These are nonprofit organizations of every kind.

.net *Network.*
> Internet and other telecommunications service providers sometimes use this, instead of .com.

.gov *Government.*
> This designates nonmilitary government branches, such as NASA, the IRS, and state governments.

.mil *Military.*
> These are for branches of the U.S. military.

The top-level domains for Web sites outside the United States are two letter abbreviations of the country name either in English (*.jp* for Japan) or in that country's language (*.de* for Deutschland, that is, Germany). Occasionally, a United States top-level domain name of *.us* will be used when confusion might otherwise be caused. For example, Canada uses the top-level domain *.ca*, which in the United States is the postal abbreviation for California. So a school district might have a Web address of *www.joneshi.k12.ca.us* to ensure clarity.

Some other domain names that help describe their sites include these:

.k12 *School or School District.*
      (could be any school, kindergarten through high school)
.cc   *Community College.*
.lib *Library.*
.state *State Government.*
.ac   *Academic*
      (European equivalent of .edu).

File Type. Most document files on the Web are written in hypertext markup language (HTML), which consists of standard text marked by a set of tags that tells your browser how to display the text. (A simple example would be that <B>*Important*</B> would tell the browser to put the word *Important* in bold face type.) For this reason, you will see that most file names have the extension .html or .htm, both abbreviations for hypertext markup language.

Other file types include these:

.exe *Executable.*
      A program file.
.asp *Active Server Page.*
      A page created on request by combining HTML and other content.
.zip *Zipped.*
      A compressed file. This can be a document, program, graphic, etc.
.gif *Graphic Interchange Format.*
      A graphic file format.
.jpg *Joint Picture Experts Group.*
      Another graphic file format.
.pdf *Portable Document Format.*
      A document in Adobe Acrobat format. This is a special file that preserves the formatting of the original document. It can reproduce on your printer very complex pages, like tax forms. Your browser may need the Adobe Acrobat Reader plug-in to view and print these documents.

Web Tip

Be careful to note whether the file name ends in .html or .htm, because the addition or omission of that one last letter will be seen as a completely different address. If you mistakenly add or omit it, the server will return a "file not found" message.

.midi *Musical Instrument Digital Interface.*
        This is a sound file.
.mov *Movie.*
        A video file.
.avi *Video.*
        Another type of video file.
.swf *Shockwave Flash.*
        A vector graphic video file.
.wav *Wave.*
        An audio file.

What Is on the Web?

What Is on the Web—For Free?

Detractors of the World Wide Web are fond of saying that "anybody can put anything on the Web," with the implication that the Web is one vast mountain of junk information, bigotry, ignorance, and pornography. While it is true the items just mentioned are out there on the Web, the important thing to remember is that "anybody" includes a lot more than kooks and perverts. Tens of thousands of smart, caring, knowledgeable individuals, countless corporations, nonprofit organizations like consumer groups, government agencies, and so on, all have Web sites. The Web is a library that never closes, a reference source of books, articles (including news, sports, weather), photographs, maps, music, video clips, and names and addresses. There is information on the Web for almost anything you can think of. Much of the material on the Web is available for free, because of personal generosity, corporate public relations, or through the advertising model (the same method that makes network television free—advertising pays for the cost of the content).

What can you find? If you want to learn how to grow and care for bromeliads, there are several sites created by experienced growers ready to give you advice. If you have ever wondered what those weird chemical names listed on your shampoo or mousse containers do, some of the manufactures who produce those chemicals host several sites that explain in detail what those ingredients do. If a friend has a strange and rare disease, there are dozens of medical information sites to look at.

Here are just some of the kinds of information available on the Web:

Art. If you are looking for a particular old master painting, a tour of a famous museum, or some examples of contemporary art, you can find them all. For a sample site, try the National Gallery of London, at *www.nationalgallery.org.uk/*

Music. With the advent of MIDI (musical instrument digital interface) keyboards, many pieces of classical and modern music have been recorded for the Web. You can even find instrumental versions of contemporary pop songs, though many are poorly performed and most, if not all, are in probable violation of copyright. (See chapter 8 on ethics for further discussion of the issues surrounding intellectual property.) For a sample site, try The Classical Music MIDI Page at *www.sciortino.net/music.html*

Government Documents. Federal and state governments post laws, proposed legislation, consumer information, research documents, and statistics to the Web. Since government sources are generally viewed as reliable, you can find a lot of useful research material on these sites. For a sample site, try the Consumer Information Center at *www.pueblo.gsa.gov*

Literature. Novels, poetry, short stories, satire and other literary expressions (including criticism and theory) are offered. Because of copyright restrictions, most of the literature (especially novels) available dates to 1912 and earlier. However, you will be able to find some works that have been posted, either into the public domain or as part of a promotion. For a sample site, try Project Gutenberg at *www.promo.net/pg*

News, Sports, Weather. What you have enjoyed on television or in the newspaper is also, for the most part, available on the Web. Many commercial news organizations have Web presences, offering the same information as on their traditional outlets. In fact, many sites offer more than what is available on their traditional outlets, because the Web eliminates the restrictions of time and space. Articles can be as long as needed to tell the whole story, and the number of photos that can be mounted is not restricted by the number of magazine pages. All of the information can be updated as often as desired (some sites

Web Tip

When you are searching for a noncomputer item that may sound like a computer-related item, be sure to specify in your search string that you do not want computers. If, for example, you are looking for information about dehydrated apple chips, recall that Apple is a computer maker and chip can refer to an integrated circuit chip.

update every few minutes, some every few hours). For a sample site, try the *New York Times* at *www.nytimes.com* (and do not forget weather at *www.weather.com* and Sports Illustrated at *www.cnnsi.com*).

Computers. The inventors of the Web, and the first few million people who began to use it, were very interested in computers and computer technology, so the Web has always had a disproportionate amount of computer information on it. For a sample site, try News.com at *www.news.com*

Library Card Catalogs. Hundreds of libraries have online card catalogs available through the Web. You can connect to the catalog and see what books and journals the library has. For a sample site, try MELVYL, the University of California Online Catalog at *www.melvyl.ucop.edu*

Corporate Information. Some corporations have what amounts to little more than advertisements on the Web, puffing their products the same way a television commercial might. Others have product catalogs, corporate financial information and lists of contacts. And many companies have additional resources, ranging from consumer tips and information for the public to detailed information about products and manufacturing processes. For a sample site, try the Gerber Web site (which includes parenting information and frequently asked questions about baby care) at *www.gerber.com*

Addresses and Phone Numbers. The Web is not always your final destination. It can be a source where you can find telephone numbers and addresses for individuals and businesses and even maps that show you how to get from your location to a destination you choose. For a sample site, try the GTE SuperPages at *superpages. gte.net*

Shopping. One of the driving forces that has caused many companies to rush to the Web is the prospect of making money directly through it.

Web Tip

Be careful about shopping online with a company you have never heard of. Most of the businesses are legitimate, but there are a few scam artists who are ready to take your money (and credit card number) and disappear. Many credit card companies guarantee your card against fraud, limiting your loss either to nothing or to $50. Check with your card issuer to learn about its policy. (Your card issuer probably has a Web site.)

Thus, there are many opportunities to shop online, for everything from books to chocolate to medical oxygen to stereo equipment. For a sample site, try shopping for books and CDs at Amazon.com at *www.amazon.com*.

What Is on the Web—For a Price?

Now we come to a critical distinction about what you can get on the Web. Information is a product that requires time, effort, and money to produce. While some corporations are willing to give information away because it serves their interest or image to do so, and while others have learned how to support information availability through online advertising, other corporations have not yet done so, and offer to sell their information to the end-user. How to recover the costs of creating and presenting information is one of the ongoing problems in the electronic world. A good example would be online newspapers. Some newspapers have their entire paper online, while others have only a few stories. Some papers have freely available archives of past issues, while others want to sell past articles at prices substantially higher than a copy of the entire original paper. As publishers experiment, what was once free may begin to cost and vice versa. For the foreseeable future, however, at least some resources on the Web will be available only for a fee. Here are some examples of commercial databases that charge a fee:

Commercial Databases. There are several proprietary databases of periodical articles, which allow you to read and print copyrighted materials for a fee. Lexis/Nexis, Infotrac, Encyclopedia Britannica, and Electric Library are some examples of companies that, in addition to the costs of maintaining a Web site, as outlined in the paragraph above, must pay license fees to the copyright holders of the information. Northern Light is a hybrid service, providing searching on the Web at large as well as on a commercial database. Users can choose to search for only free Web sites or for the fee-based articles.

What Is Not on the Web?

There are billions of dollars' worth of copyrighted intellectual property in the world, in the form of books, movies, music, articles in periodicals, photographs, and the like. Those who make a living by creating and marketing these works must be able to receive income from them in some way. While an increasing number of magazine and journal articles are available on the Web, either free, for a per use fee, or for a subscription fee, few book publishers have discovered how to charge for reading books online, so most of the books in a typical bookstore or library are not available free on the Web, nor are many other items like commercial releases of popular music. Further, millions of copyrighted but out-of-print books exist which would need to be put into digital form in order to be made available on the Web even for a fee. (And millions of books out of copyright still wait to be put into digital form as well.) Photographs and art-works would need to be scanned, and privately owned databases would have to be converted to Web-friendly format. Magazines and journals with only a small circulation may not have a Web presence, and to read an article in one of them you would have to go to the printed version.

Useful Features of Your Browser

Just as various software manufacturers make competing word pro-cessing or spreadsheet programs, they also make competing browsers, those application programs that allow you to access the Web. Whether you are using Netscape Navigator or Microsoft's Internet Explorer, your browser has several features that will help you work with the Web more effectively. The term *browser* comes from the days of mostly text-based files. The browser software allowed a user to request a file and then browse through it to see whether it suited the user's need. Now that most Web pages contain hyperlinks leading to various other sites, the operational metaphor is surfing—moving from site to site rapidly, riding the wave of personal interest to find the ultimate site.

The Netscape Navigator tool bar provides the "Bookmark" option on the lower left of the screen.

Bookmarks

A bookmark, called a "Favorite" in Internet Explorer, is simply a saved URL in a file. When you find a Web site you might want to return to, you can simply add the URL to the bookmark file. It is saved by the title of the page so you can remember its topic. To add a bookmark, choose "Bookmarks," then click on "Add Bookmark" from the menu.

If you use a university computer, or if you move from computer to computer, you may not want to save the bookmarks permanently on the computer you are using. Instead, you can save the file to a floppy disk (using the extension *.htm* (as in: *search98.htm*). When you have finished a session, you can go to the bookmark file (choose "Bookmarks" or "Favorites"), then "Go to Bookmarks" and then click on "File," click on "Save As" and the file will be saved to your floppy disk. Later on, or at another computer, put your floppy disk in the computer, go to the book- mark file and choose "File," then "Open File" and use the bookmarks on the new browser. Be sure to delete the bookmarks you have added to the school's browser in each case before you leave. (But do not delete any bookmarks the school has put there.)

Your saved bookmark file can be taken from computer to computer and even copied to give to a friend or turned in with the research project you have completed.

If you do have your own computer, you can not only save bookmarks into folders to organize them by category, but you can annotate them as well. If you go to the book- mark file, choose a bookmark, and then choose "Properties," you will see the bookmark name, the actual URL, and an area where you can type in a description or note about the site. Note that the Properties information also includes the date when the bookmark was added and the date the page was last visited.

Internet Explorer provides the bookmarking function from the top of the tool bar.

History File

More recent versions of Netscape and Internet Explorer contain a list of all the sites visited until a preset expiration date. The length of time before expiration can be set from "expire immediately" to many days (999 in Netscape). If you are using a college-owned computer, do not reset the expiration date. The "History" file is useful for going back a number of pages (many more than you will find listed in the "Go" menu), if you have visited a few dozen during your searching session. If you own a computer, your history file will give you a record of your browsing back a week or two or more, depending on the setting.

Find In Page

This command, as an icon on the Tool Bar and on the Edit menu in both browsers, allows you to search the currently displayed page for a word or phrase. If your search engine has brought up a very long page, you may not know where on that page your search terms are located. Use this command to find them quickly.

View Page Info

This command, on the "View" menu in Netscape will give you the date the currently displayed page was last saved and the page size. This information can be useful for determining the recency of the information, especially if no date is given in the page as displayed.

Web Tip

Remember that you can simply cut and paste pieces out of a Web page, without having to save or print the entire page. If you do take material this way, be sure to include the page URL with the material and indicate clearly that the material is a quotation, so that you do not later confuse it with your own work.

Save As

You can save an entire Web page to disk by using the "Save As" command from the "File" menu. Be sure to save the file as an html document and give the file name the extension *.htm* or *.html*. When you want to view the page again, use the "File," "Open File" choice and the file will load just as if you were online. Do note that the embedded images in the file are actually separate files, so you must save each one separately in the same directory as the html page if you wish to see the images. To save an image from a Web page, right click on it (for Windows; for Mac click and hold down the button), and then choose "Save File As" and save it to your disk, keeping the extension (*.jpg* or *.gif*) of the original file. The correct extension will be added automatically as long as you do not add another of your own.

Anatomy of a Web Site

Every Web site has a main page (called a Home Page or a start page) that serves to identify the site owner and offers either a table of contents or a set of graphics (buttons or pictures) to let the user navigate the site.

The main page will contain some or all of these pieces:

Title Graphic

This graphic file often contains the corporate logo, announcing the site owner. In addition, part of the graphic may include a navigation bar with choices (such as search, help, etc.).

Banner Advertisement

Many sites derive operating revenue from advertising, so a first and prominent kind of advertising is the banner advertisement often stretching all across the screen. Many of these now make use of animated *.gif* files, which gives them movement. The ads themselves nearly always have embedded hyperlinks, so that you can click the mouse in the ad area and go directly to the advertiser's site for more information. (Some sites get paid when you merely look at the ad when the page comes up—these are called views—while others get paid only when you click on the ad itself to see what the advertiser has to say—these are called click throughs.)

Web Tip

To learn whether a hyperlink will take you to another site or to another page within the same site, move the mouse pointer over the link but do not click on it. Then look at the bottom of the screen and you will see the destination address revealed.

Search Button

Many large sites have their own search capability, allowing you to look for specific pieces of information on the site. If the home page does not contain a link or directory listing that seems likely to include the information you want, you can search the site by keyword.

Hyperlinks

Almost all home pages contain links to other pages. Many of these links will be to other pages on the site, while some may be links to other sites. When you move your mouse pointer over a hyperlink, but before you click on it, you can see at the bottom of your browser window the address where the link will take you.

Frames

Frames divide your browser screen into two or more independent sections, so that one section can be changed or scrolled while the other(s) remain the same. (Each frame can be scrolled independently of the other.) Some sites use frames to display an index or menu in one area while another frame displays the information selected from the menu.

Some sites that use frames allow a user to choose a "no frames" version, either because the user's browser does not support frames, or because the user does not like them. (There is even a "no frames" campaign on the Web, spread by users who believe that frames are clumsy and awkward, requiring constant scrolling, back and forth and up and down, inside several cramped spaces on the screen.)

Web Tip

If you want to print from a page with frames, first click your mouse pointer in the frame you want to print. Each frame is actually a separate file, so you must select the one you want to print before clicking on the print button.

Footer Area

At the bottom of the page, whether a home page or daughter page, the site owner will often place information relating to corporate ownership, copyright, contact information, related links, and other information. You may also find a date of page creation or last change, which can be helpful for judging the currency of the information on the page.

Columns

As an alternative to frames, the page may be divided into columns, with a narrower left-hand column containing an index or directory of the site and a wider right-hand column containing the main information for the page. Or you may discover three columns. Various background colors in each column may serve to separate them from

one another, so that the information does not look like a table.

Images

An image is a graphic representation or picture of something. An image can be a drawing, a photograph, or even a graphic representation of text characters. Many headlines on Web pages are graphic images because the page creators want to use unusual fonts not available on the Web browser. Some graphics in the *.gif* format show several images in rapid sequence, so that they appear to show motion. These are called animated gifs.

Plug-Ins

Some Web sites contain special formatting or presentation features or special file types that require helper programs before a browser can display, play, or print them. These helper programs, called plug-ins, are usually available free (though more sophisticated versions are also for sale).

Some of the more common plug-ins are these:

Acrobat Reader. This helper enables a browser to display and print files in the .pdf format. These files retain much more sophisticated formatting than a Web browser can support by itself. A free version is available from Adobe *www.adobe.com*

Quick Time. This helper enables a browser to play video clips stored in the Quick Time format. A free version is available from Apple *www.apple.com*

Real Player. This helper enables a browser to play Real Audio files (if the computer is also equipped with a sound card and speakers or earphones) and Real Video files. A free version is available from Real Corp. *www.real.com*

Shockwave Flash. This helper enables a browser to view streaming vector graphic video from the Web site. A free version is available from *www.macromedia.com*

Web Tip

Many of the more common plug-ins are being pre-installed in the newer versions of both Netscape and Internet Explorer, so you may not need to download one or more of them, if you have a current browser release. If you use a school computer, the plug-ins may have been added already. If not, be sure to get permission before attempting to add a plug-in.

Questions about Access Problems to Web Sites

Q When I try to log onto a Web site, I get the message, "Access Forbidden," or "Access Denied."

Several situations can result in a message like this. At some sites, if you attempt to go to a particular directory but do not include a file name, this message lets you know that you are not authorized to see the directory itself. A message like this will also appear if you attempt to visit a commercial site that allows access from only specific addresses. (For example, if your library subscribes to an online database, it can be accessed only from library computers that are "calling" from one of several specific IP (Internet Protocol) addresses. A final possibility is that the site is an adult site that requires a preauthorized procedure to enter.

Q When I click on a link, I get the message, "Error 404: Not Found."

This message is returned when a particular file cannot be found on the host server. There are four possible reasons. (1) You mistyped the filename, so that indeed no such file exists on the server. (2) The file has been moved to another directory. (3) The file has been removed from the server. (4) The file has expired (some files have expiration dates in them). Some servers have more elaborate messages than the bare-bones default message, so you may see a polite version of the 404 message instead ("We're sorry—we cannot find the file you requested.")

Q When I try to visit a page, a dialog box comes up that asks for a user ID and password.

Some sites are password-protected. This does not necessarily mean that they charge to use the site, but some kind of registration is required. Sometimes a site will be set up for the purpose of serving a restricted audience, whose members are given the user ID and password. (Some textbook publishers do this, for example.)

Q In place of an image on a page, my browser shows a broken square with a question mark in it.

The page your browser is displaying names an image to be displayed in that spot, but the server for some reason did not send the image along. You might click on the Reload button to see if the image is sent on a new try. Sometimes, however, the problem lies with the host server.

Q The site I want to visit requires registration, but it is free. Why do I have to register if using the site is free?

Many site owners want more than just a list of anonymous visitors to their sites. They would like to know how often the same person visits, how long the visit lasts, and what pages are viewed in what order. For this reason, the owners request or require registration. An additional feature of registration is that you can be welcomed by name when you visit, and any preferences you have indicated can be put into effect ("Take me right to news, but no sports," for example). The site can do this by setting a cookie on your browser. (A cookie is a line of letters and numbers, stored in the file *cookies.txt* on your hard drive, that tells the host about you when you connect to it. The host computer itself does not store this information.)

Q When I try to visit a site, I get the message, "Unable to locate the server. The server does not have a DNS entry."

The hardware of the net (servers, routers, and so forth) communicates by using addresses expressed by strings of numbers. So when you type in the name of a site you want to visit, that name is first sent to a Domain Name Server (DNS), which looks it up and finds the numerical address corresponding to it. If the DNS cannot find the site name in its index, you receive the message above. The possibilities are, in order of likelihood, (1) you simply mistyped the URL, (2) your network connection is down temporarily, or (3) the host server is no longer online or not yet online.

Q When I try to visit a site, I get the message, "The server is not responding. It may be down or busy," or "Network connection refused by server."

Either one of these messages tells you that the server does indeed exist and have a DNS entry (see above), but that it is not responding to the request to send the files you want. Try rerequesting by clicking on Stop and then Reload. If this does not work, wait a few minutes and try again.

Q When I try to visit a page, the page loads partly and then seems to stall.

If the site loads slowly but continues to load, you are merely enjoying the World Wide Wait, a common phenomenon when the Net itself or the server you are accessing gets overly busy. If the page stalls for more than twenty seconds, try clicking on Stop and then Reload. A new request often gets faster response as a new set of packets follows a different route from the host to your browser.

✶ Chapter 3 ✶

Searching the Web I: Search Tools

Using Search Tools

Search tools make up a group of Web sites that help you to find information (including documents, images, sounds and more) on the Web, either by collecting and organizing sites into subject directories or by sending out powerful software programs (spiders) to read and index large portions of the Web. Almost every tool has special features, and even tools that appear to cover the same function may have different methods of ranking hits, and they may cover different areas of the Web.

A good first step in preparing to find information on the Web would be to familiarize yourself with the various kinds of tools available, to understand their different functions, special features, and methods of operation. When you are presented with a research problem, you will be both more confident and more successful if you know you have a whole toolkit of varied tools with which to work.

This chapter covers the major tools, including search engines, directories, and specialty tools, and describes a few lesser-known but handy additional search resources as well. An informative way to get comfortable with these tools is to take the same search phrase to several of them in order to see the different results and to compare how those results are presented. You will notice that some tools give you the date of each document found, while others do not. Is date important to you for this search? What about size? Do you want to find sites that have been rated by the search service? Do you need to begin with a broader topic search and then search within it to narrow your initial results, in order to focus your topic? Whatever your needs at the time, a little experience with these tools will enable you to choose the right ones for a given task.

Tool Types

Traditionally (which, for the Web, means a few years ago), there were three general categories of search tool: search engines (like AltaVista and HotBot), directories (like Yahoo and Magellan), and specialty tools (like the SuperPages or DejaNews). Today, however, the distinctions are becoming less clear, as many search sites have metamorphosed into super sites by constantly adding features, making agreements with other search tools, and buying each other. Many tools now want to be perceived as portals—your gateway to everything on the Web—so that you will use them as your start page or at least visit them frequently (the "one-stop-shopping" syndrome for cyberspace).

Most search tools are owned by commercial enterprises interested in making money through advertising. The more often you (and millions of others) use a given search tool, the more revenue is generated for the search tool company. Knowing this, you will not be surprised that, through the fundamental law of competition, many of the search tools are constantly reinventing themselves, adding some features and deleting others in an effort to encourage you to visit them more often. Thus, what used to be "just a search engine" may now also offer a subject directory, news headlines, free software, telephone and e-mail directories, stock quotations, and even airline reservations—not to mention more and more "buying opportunities," in the form of multiple advertisements. Do not be surprised, then, if from one visit to the next to a particular tool, you discover one feature gone and two more added. Such is the nature of change in cyberspace.

Even though the addition of features is creating some blurring of the lines, the concepts of search engine, directory, and specialty site

Search Tip

Be careful not to get in the rut of always going to the same tool, or even of thinking about a tool in a fixed way. Most of the tools add features and capability regularly. By visiting various tools from time to time, you will maintain a current feel for the varying strengths of each.

are still relevant for understanding how the types of tool and their searches work.

Search Engines

When you type in some keywords into a search engine, the engine compares them with a huge index it has compiled from visiting Web pages out on the Internet. The engine visits Web pages by means of a program called a spider (or robot, bot, or crawler), that travels all over the Web reading the sites it locates and sending back the words for indexing. Some spiders read every word on every page located, while others read only the first part of the page or even just the metatags (special lines containing keywords just for spiders).

Hundreds of search sites exist on the Web, though many are either small or merely links to the major engines and directories. Later in this chapter you will find a discussion of the major engines.

When you are choosing and using search engines, then, remember these facts:

- ✶ No single engine can read the entire Web. The largest ones have indexed only about one third of the Web.
- ✶ The more information on a page read by the engine, the more different words will be indexed from that page.
- ✶ The larger the database of the engine, the more hits you are likely to get from a given set of keywords.
- ✶ The engine returns hits found in its index, not necessarily currently on the Web. You will therefore sometimes get an error message ("404: Not Found" or something similar) when you click on a link to go to a page that is no longer mounted on the Web. Indexes take awhile to remove dead links.
- ✶ The content of the Web is in constant flux with thousands of pages being added daily and thousands of others being removed. No engine can keep completely up-to-date with this activity. Which engine has the "freshest" content is a matter of great competitive debate.
- ✶ Search engines run their spiders constantly, so new material is added every day. A search on Wednesday may find more information than did a search on Monday.

Directories

A directory is a hierarchical subject guide of sites chosen by the editors of the directory site or recommend to them by others. Most directories begin with a dozen or two general subject areas, such as arts, computers, family, health, and so forth. Then, beneath each general area is a collection of subcategories, each of which has another set of subcategories. This arrangement allows the user to "drill down" to a more refined subject area, until a set of pertinent links is revealed. Many directories allow searches as well as the drill-down method of finding subject-specific links.

When choosing and using a directory, keep in mind the following:

✫ Some directories describe each site in summary form, while others offer evaluations of quality for each site.
✫ Criteria for ranking and for quality evaluation vary from directory to directory.
✫ Criteria for inclusion and the degree of personal assessment vary from directory to directory.
✫ For some directories the search takes place on the directory database itself, while for others the search is connected to a search engine database of the Web. Check the information on the directory site—either on the home page or in the "Help" or "About" choices—so that you will know just what you are going to be searching.

Specialty Tools

These tools include regional search engines (engines covering Web sites in particular geographic locations), subject-specific search engines (such as law or medicine), metasearch tools (for sending a query to several search engines at once) and tools for finding residential or retail addresses, e-mail addresses, phone numbers, Zip codes, toll-free phone numbers, maps, and the like. Knowing about some of the more common specialty tools can help speed up a search.

Search Tool Ranking Issues

There are two issues to be aware of when you view the rankings of the hits in a search tool. (The ranking is the order in which the hits are listed.) First is the variation in ranking between different tools. Each search tool has its own set of rules for ranking sites. Generally speaking, for search engines, the more times a keyword occurs on a page and the closer together the keywords are, the higher the ranking of that page will be. But the exact method varies. Good advice, then, is to change engines if your keywords fail to present you with some likely hits near the top of the list. You might be surprised to see the same keywords produce an entirely different set of hits on another engine.

The second issue relates to the intentional manipulation of keywords by the producer of the Web page to produce a higher position on the ranking list. Studies of users show that most people look at the first ten or perhaps twenty hits in a search and ignore the rest. The creators of some sales sites therefore take steps to help their site land in the top ten or twenty by sometimes repeating certain keywords dozens or even hundreds of times on their page, sometimes at the end of their advertisement and also by sometimes using white text on a white background (so that you cannot see it, though the search engine spider can). Such word-stuffing practices are called spamming or spamdexing, named after the Hormel meat product Spam, which was featured with every meal in a Monty Python comedy skit. Some of the engines now use antispam tests to detect and reject such pages, but you should be aware of this practice and not take rankings in too absolute a way.

The Major Search Engines

This section is presented in a handy reference format, with the list arranged in order of power and importance rather than alphabetically, so that you can easily choose the tools appropriate for your particular searches.

AltaVista
www.altavista.com

Description: AltaVista has a very large database based on full-text searches of Web pages. Even though it is one of the most powerful and comprehensive search engines available, search results are returned very quickly.

As with other search tools, AltaVista is positioning itself as a hub or portal, so it is adding "zones" and "services" and even directory features as well as its search functions. Usenet newsgroups can also be searched from AltaVista.

Recommended for:
- ★ Very specific terms (such as chemical names or diseases)
- ★ Obscure pieces of information
- ★ Long or unusual exact phrases

☆ Complex keyword searches

☆ Extensive or serious research projects

Features of Note:

☆ Identify keywords as "must include" (with a plus sign), "must not include" (with a minus sign), and "may include" (the keyword with no sign): *+rafting –whitewater river*

☆ Exact phrase searches by using quotation marks: *"Leaning Tower of Pisa"*

☆ Field identifiers to restrict searches to particular fields: *title: "the froggy page"*

☆ Wild cards with asterisk: *Fortun** to find *fortune, fortunately, fortunate,* etc.

☆ Case sensitive search by using capital letters: *john* returns *john* or *John,* but *John* returns only *John*

☆ Advanced search supports full Boolean: AND, OR, AND NOT, NEAR, as well as nesting and searching within a range of dates (See chapter 4, p. 45 for discussion of Boolean Operators.)

☆ A subject directory is available by clicking on "Browse Categories."

Hit List Features:

☆ Date last modified given for each document (so you can check timeliness)

☆ Size of each document listed in kilobytes (so you can judge comparative length)

Overall: AltaVista is a very powerful tool, especially if you control your searches with the various delimiters available. As long as you enter several words (most important ones first) and are not intimidated by large numbers of hits, you will usually be successful even as a beginner.

HotBot
www.hotbot.com

Description: HotBot is the second of the two largest database search engines. Pull-down menus (menus that drop down from a menu bar when the mouse is clicked on the drop-down arrow to the right of the bar or on the initial word when there is no drop-down arrow) make customized searching easy. You can select the return of more than ten results at a time (up to 100). Supports searches of Web and Usenet newsgroups.

Recommended for:

☆ Beginners and experienced searchers who want an extensive database

- ★ Very specific terms
- ★ Obscure pieces of information
- ★ Searches restricted by region or recency (last week, month, etc.)

Features of Note:
- ★ Subsearch allows you to search within the previous set of results
- ★ Search Options permit extensive customization and field searches
- ★ Control the depth of search within each Web site
- ★ Some directory content is available

Hit List Features:
- ★ Each hit is given a confidence ranking in percent

Overall: AltaVista and HotBot are the two premier engines for depth searching. HotBot is a little easier to use because of the pull-down menus. Both cover somewhat different content and have different ranking schemes, so that using them together can be a real benefit.

Northern Light
www.northernlight.com

Description: Northern Light is a large Web database with an additional database of periodical articles available for a fee. NL says this special collection consists of "4,500 journals, reviews, books, magazines, and newswires not readily found on the Web." Cost is based on use.

Recommended for:
- ★ Exact phrase searches
- ★ Scholarly topics
- ★ Topics likely to be in professional journals

Features of Note:
- ★ Engine creates custom search folders by subtopic to help narrow search automatically
- ★ WWW and Special Collection (for fee) hits clearly differentiated by labels

Search Tip

Remember that even though you may receive thousands of hits from one of the major engines, there are not necessarily thousands of relevant documents. For example, a search on three keywords will return a hit for any page that contains any one of those keywords anywhere in the document. The most relevant documents (with the keywords closer together) should be near the front of the hit list.

✶ Boolean AND, OR, NOT are supported, as well as plus, minus, exact phrase in quotation marks and wildcards. Field searching also supported (e.g. title: *"Procter & Gamble"*).

✶ Glossary of Internet terms (under "Help")

Hit List Features:

✶ Confidence ranking in percent for each hit

✶ Date of page given for each hit

✶ Engine displays 25 hits per screen

Overall: Even if you use only the free Web search, Northern Light is an excellent resource, with a lot of fresh content. Often the newest information seems to be here first. And first hits often seem more relevant to keywords here than with the two larger engines discussed above.

Excite
www.excite.com

Description: The Excite search engine has a medium-sized database, and includes current news articles from more than 300 periodicals. Excite also includes a directory, with recommended sites listed first.

Recommended for:

✶ Current events and topics involving politics, society, culture

✶ Working a topic down from more general to more specific

✶ Accessing a general subject (like astronomy) for a handful of recommended sites

Features of Note:

✶ Concept searching allows the engine to search beyond your exact terms for related ideas (a search on *rain* will bring hits related to weather)

✶ Power search allows search customization and up to 50 hits to be returned per page

✶ Boolean AND, OR, AND NOT, quotation marks, plus, minus

✶ Reference tools (yellow pages, e-mail, stock quotes, etc.)

Hit List Features:

✶ Check boxes with related words are provided to allow narrowing a search

✶ Percentage relevancy rankings

✶ "Search for more documents like this one" choice after each hit to allow refinement of your search

✶ News article and directory matches as well as general Web hits

Overall: Excite is a very handy tool if you are not sure whether you need a directory or a search engine and when you want to play with a topic for awhile to identify your exact interest.

Infoseek
www.infoseek.go.com

Description: Infoseek is a combination directory and search engine, allowing you to attack your search interest either from a topical standpoint or from a keyword search. You can search not only the Web, but also recent news stories, Usenet newsgroups, and a database of corporate profiles.

Recommended for:
- ⭐ Current events in the news
- ⭐ A mix of recommended sites and general Web search hits
- ⭐ One keyword searching (e.g. *airlines*) using "Extra Search Precision" function

Features of Note:
- ⭐ Results grouping returns only one hit per site, rather than a hit for every occurrence of terms
- ⭐ Lists recommended sites (from its directory) first, then general search hits
- ⭐ News headlines, yellow pages, maps, stock information, dictionary, thesaurus also available by clicking
- ⭐ Able to search within results of a search in order to refine a query
- ⭐ Supports quotation marks for exact phrases, plus and minus for "must include" and "must exclude"
- ⭐ Supports plain English queries (*Where can I find a list of amusement parks?*)
- ⭐ Supports field searches (*title: "Vicar of Wakefield"*)
- ⭐ Advanced search available for customizing search expressions

Hit List Features:
- ⭐ Relevancy rating in percentages
- ⭐ Document date
- ⭐ Document size
- ⭐ "See more pages from this site" option

Overall: The total package, including search speed, grouping, site ratings and document date and size make Infoseek a very useful tool either for a quick check of a subject or as a starting place for research.

Lycos
www.lycos.com

Description: Like so many other search tools, Lycos is a combination search engine and directory. One of its features is its "Top 5 percent" directory of sites the editors have chosen as among the best on the Web. Searches can focus on the general Web, the "Top 5 percent" sites, newsgroups, Reuters news, weather, a dictionary, pictures, sounds, GTE yellow pages, and recipes.

Recommended for:
- ★ Locating sites that have been rated highly by reviewers
- ★ Locating pictures and images

Features of Note:
- ★ "Picture This" image search
- ★ "Lycos Pro" feature has easy-to-use advanced search options
- ★ Supports searches on Web page titles
- ★ Can search a selected Web site only
- ★ Supports exact phrase, "must include," and "must exclude" with quotation marks, plus, and minus
- ★ Supports rich Boolean with AND, OR, NOT, ADJ, NEAR, FAR, BEFORE

Hit List Features:
- ★ "More Like This" selection
- ★ Option to search within results for narrowing search

Overall: Lycos is excellent for finding highly rated sites and for finding images. It has a very full set of Boolean operators.

The Major Directories

Yahoo
www.yahoo.com

Description: Yahoo is the oldest and best-known directory on the Web. Its catalog is small compared with the search engines, but the content is very good and well organized. For a topical "drill-down" approach to a subject, it is still among the very best.

Recommended for:
- ★ Searching for sites by subject or academic area
- ★ Narrowing a subject by examining the possibilities in a directory
- ★ Finding lists of resources (such as colleges, medical sites, newspapers)

Features of Note:

* ⭐ Excellent "Reference" category (missing from many directories)
* ⭐ "Drill down" through the directories or search the catalog by keyword
* ⭐ Regional Yahoos available for several foreign countries
* ⭐ "Full Coverage" news section for collecting many stories on major current events
* ⭐ Search options provide for AND, OR, exact phrase, and recency

Hit List Features:

* ⭐ Site matches and category matches listed separately

Overall: Even though it does not present site descriptions, Yahoo is still one of the most popular search tools.

Galaxy
galaxy.tradewave.com

Description: More than some other directories, Galaxy appears to be designed for searchers of scholarly subject matter, calling itself "The professional's guide to a world of information." Galaxy's main entries, especially in engineering, law, medicine, and social science, seem geared toward the serious rather than the recreational searcher.

Recommended for:

* ⭐ Science and health-related research
* ⭐ Academic research

Features of Note:

* ⭐ Directory entries in a category are conveniently broken down into Academic Organizations, Announcements, Articles, Books, Collections, and several other sub-categories.
* ⭐ Supports search on the directory, using Boolean, quotation marks, and wild cards.

Hit List Features:

* ⭐ Using the advanced search function produces a hit list that includes relevancy ranking, document size, dates entered and indexed, a helpful excerpt, a list of frequent words in the document, and a document outline.

Overall: Galaxy is a small directory, but has some very useful features in its search function. This would be a good place to start for a general academic subject.

Magellan
www.mckinley.com

Description: A search engine and directory combination, Magellan allows a user to search on the entire Web (meaning Magellan's medium-sized database), reviewed sites only (60,000), and Green Light sites only (sites reviewed and approved as suitable for families).

Recommended for:
- ✶ Searching for sites that have been reviewed
- ✶ Approaching a topic by both keyword search and directory "drill down"
- ✶ Searching for a topic that may include a keyword used by "adult" sites. Selecting Green Light sites only will exclude the adult sites. (For example, searching for the topic *young girls' sports* under an entire Web search yields many "adult" sites, while using a Green Light search produces only sites actually related to sports for young girls.)

Features of Note:
- ✶ Green Light sites
- ✶ Supports Boolean AND, OR, AND NOT, as well as plus and minus for must "include" and "must exclude"

Hit List Features:
- ✶ Relevance ranking in percent
- ✶ "Find Similar" option to further refine search
- ✶ Site summaries (most engines offer site summaries, while most directories do not)

Overall: Very good for reviewed sites and for using Green Light sites to filter unwanted hits.

LookSmart
www.looksmart.com

Description: LookSmart is a fairly large directory (600,000 sites), with a full Web search provided by a link to AltaVista. In the directory results, the sites judged best are listed first, and then the remainder are listed alphabetically.

Recommended for:
- ✶ General directory usage (searching by subject)

Features of Note:
- ✶ Unique directory format makes searching, backing up, moving around in categories very easy and intuitive
- ✶ Clickable tabs take the user to a "people finder" and discussion groups.
- ✶ A link to fee-based content at Electric Library

Hit List Features:
    ★ File size and date are given.
Overall: LookSmart is an outstanding directory that would be a good first choice for subject searches.

eBLAST
www.ebig.com

Description: eBLAST is a directory of 125,000 rated and reviewed Web sites from the Encyclopaedia Britannica corporation.
Recommended for:
    ★ Finding Web sites at multiple levels of specificity (from general to specific)
    ★ Locating highly rated Web sites
    ★ Academic research in most subject areas
Features of Note:
    ★ Search the directory by keyword
    ★ Add AltaVista database search to directory search
    ★ Find sites at each directory level
    ★ Get information about each site's owner
Hit List Features:
    ★ Each site rated from one to five stars and ranked by rating
    ★ Summaries are evaluative of the site, not just descriptions
    ★ Elegant presentation of current location in directory levels
Overall: eBLAST is one of the newer directories, but shows a fine sense of selectivity and features many high quality sites.

WebCrawler
www.webcrawler.com

Description: WebCrawler is a small but useful directory with search capability. It features an especially good reference section.
Recommended for:
    ★ An additional directory tool for general subject searches
Features of Note:
    ★ Includes yellow pages, maps, people finder
    ★ Supports Boolean AND, OR, NOT, and plus, minus, and quotation marks for "must include," "must not include," and "exact phrase"
    ★ Product finder for locating consumer goods
Hit List Features:
    ★ The default (initial setting) is to list titles only. Summaries can be shown by selecting them
    ★ Showing summaries also shows relevancy ranking and "Similar Pages" choice

Overall: WebCrawler is another choice in the combination directory and search engine category.

Specialty Tools

Argus Clearinghouse
www.clearinghouse.net

Description: Argus describes itself as a "collection of topical guides," something of a directory of directories. Search by subject, as with a regular directory, except you'll find a list of directories to resources at the end, rather than a list of documents. Each directory is rated according to how well the resources are described and evaluated. The directory is also searchable, with hits check-rated from one to five checks.

Recommended for: Argus is a good resource for general subject areas likely to have multiple directories covering them (chemistry, boating, diseases, famous historical events).

InfoSpace
www.infospace.com

Description: InfoSpace is a collection of online directories, including yellow pages, white pages (for residential and e-mail addresses), government information, and, for a fee, public records.

Recommended for: Excellent for locating people, businesses, products, or phone numbers.

DejaNews
www.dejanews.com

Description: This is an archive of searchable Usenet newsgroup discussions, dating back to 1995. You can search by keyword for postings in one category or all categories. There are thousands of newsgroups, many with hundreds of new postings each day, resulting in a very large database of information.

Recommended for: Information and opinion, and sometimes contact information for people knowledgeable in specific areas, are available here. Large sections of the newsgroups are wastelands of rumor, gossip, irrational name-calling, and outright misinformation, but there is much useful information here as well. Be cautious.

Liszt
www.liszt.com

Description: Liszt is a directory of more than 90,000 electronic mailing lists. Mailing lists can be located by subject from a directory or by searching.

Recommended for: Finding a list related to your research subject: you can receive current discussion information and even ask questions of the list members.

The Great American Web Site
www.uncle-sam.com

Description: Great American is a gateway to U.S. federal government Web sites from all branches and agencies. Whether you need the Web site of the CIA, the Library of Congress, or the National Endowment for the Arts, you can click on their index entries here.

Recommended for: Finding legislation, statistics, and information from government agencies (agriculture, labor, education, transportation, etc.).

Search Tools for Special Questions

Here are several special tools that will help you solve particular search problems.

1. Find a company's site. If you want to search for a particular company or for an entire site (rather than just a page) covering a subject, try Thunderstone at *search.thunderstone.com*

2. Perform metasearching. Metasearching is the action of searching on several of the major engines all at the same time. To do this, try Dogpile at *www.dogpile.com* or Mamma at *mamma.com* or Metacrawler at *www.metacrawler.com*

3. Find search engines for one subject. To search by subject area (such as Science), try Beaucoup at *www.beaucoup.com,* or DirectoryGuide at *www.directoryguide.com,* or SuperSeek at *www.super-seek.com*

4. Find search engines for a geographical region. To find an engine that covers a specific country, try E-directory at *www.edirectory.com*

5. Search in plain English. To perform a natural language search (by simply typing in the question you want answered), try Ask Jeeves at *www.askjeeves.com*

6. Find a Web ring. Web rings are collections of sites that are associated with each other because they cover the same subject. You can move easily from site to site by using the navigation buttons on each one. To find Web rings by subject, try WebRing at *www.webring.org*

7. Check the encyclopedia. To find a brief encyclopedia entry for an author, event, or subject, try Encyclopedia.com at *www.encyclopedia.com* or Encarta Online at *encarta.msn.com/EncartaHome.asp*

★ Chapter 4 ★

Searching the Web II: Search Strategies

Preparing to Search

An old rule of thumb tells us to "spend five percent of your time to plan the other ninety-five percent." This rule can serve you well with your Web searching. Take a few minutes to plan your search strategy and you will find that searching is not only faster but more productive as well. Here are some ideas for effective planning:

Frame Your Problem in Terms of Information Needs

The first step toward effective searching is to define your problem using the concepts or phrases that might appear in the answer. That is, you must go beyond the question of what you want to know and think how the issue might be described. For example, suppose you have the question, "Is the family in trouble?" How might this issue be approached? Would the answer be found in a discussion of what makes marriages last, or in an article on declining birth rates in industrialized countries?

You also must consider what kind of information will be able to answer your question, so that you will know where to look. As in the example, "Is the family in trouble?" should you look at marriage and divorce rates, statistics on child abuse or alcoholism, inventories of marital happiness, single-parent families, or some other topic? The answers here will suggest looking at various databases (perhaps government statistics), social science sites, or perhaps even historical discussions of family life.

Another way to help plan your search is to ask, "How will I know when I have found the answer?" "What is it likely to look like?" The answers to these questions should generate some creative approaches.

A very useful practice is to express your search problem in terms of the key concepts you can derive from it. You might list these concepts across the top of a piece of paper or word processor file. Then, beneath each concept, list synonymous words or phrases. These words will help you construct several different search strings if you discover that the original concept words are not yielding the desired results.

As you create additional key concepts for your search, move up and down the ladder of generalization. For example, if you are searching for information about cosmetic ingredients, move up the ladder to some more general concepts such as chemicals or chemical manufacturers, and then down the ladder to some specific examples, such as dimethicone or carnauba wax.

Select Research Sources That Will Fill Your Information Needs

The second step in planning your search is to ask, "Where is the information identified in step one the most likely to be found?" As we discussed in the chapter on search tools, there are directories for general topics, general search engines for phrase and keyword searches, specialized search engines, and specialized sites. For example, if you are researching a medical issue, one of the medicine-specific sites such as Medline (*igm.nlm.nih.gov*), HealthAtoZ (*www.healthatoz.com*), Medsite (*www.medsite.com*), or Healthfinder (*www.healthfinder.com*) would be clear choices. Current events will be in the online newspapers and magazines, while historical events will be at sites devoted to history, such as the Civil War site.

Developing Search Strategies

The next step is to think about how you want to proceed with your search. Where are you going to look first? What kinds of sources will you look at (articles, statistics, online news sources)? How important is recency? Is the

Search Tip

If you are dealing with a general topic or a topic related to a well-known historical character, go to an online encyclopedia. The brief articles available will often suggest terms used in a discussion or an approach that you can then convert into search terms. You might check Encyclopedia.com (*www. encyclopedia.com*), Encarta Online (*encarta.msn.com/ EncartaHome.asp*), Encyberpedia (*www. encyberpedia.com/ency. htm*), the Free Internet Encyclopedia (*clever.net/ cam/encyclopedia.html*), and the WWW Virtual Library (*vlib.stanford. edu/Overview.html*).

information of the type that changes rapidly, or is older information valuable as well? Therefore, how far back will you go in your search? How many references will you look through? What synonyms or search strings will you use to search with?

You must make choices about how and where and how long you look, and about what you do with the information you find. What strategies will you use to comb through your findings? Skimming, paging, looking at indexes, reading first sentences, headings, abstracts? Do remember that few people can find everything of importance in just five or ten minutes. Take your searching seriously, work effectively, and in just an hour or so you should have a wealth of information.

Choosing Your Search Tools

Use Multiple Tools

Perhaps you have heard of the man with the hearty appetite who sat down in a restaurant and picked up the menu. After studying each page carefully, he finally handed it back to the waiter and said, "Yes." Now, while we normally choose only one or two items from a menu, when you are searching the Web you have permission to choose several of the available tools. The Web continues to grow at a staggering pace. Hundreds of millions of pages are now mounted, and new pages are added twenty-four hours a day. The volume and growth of the Web means that, in spite of their constant efforts, even the best search tools have indexed less than a third of available content. The good news is that different tools have indexed different parts of the Web, so that by using several tools, you can greatly increase your thoroughness of coverage.

Another reason for using several tools in

Search Tip

Use the thesaurus on your word processor to help you find synonyms for the terms you have in mind. Remember that while you may be thinking about *nutrition*, some of those writing about the topic might be using the words *diet* or *nutriment* instead.

Search Tip

Go the Websitez search engine (*www.websitez. com*) and try typing in the general subject area of your search (medicine, economics, ecology) and see if there are sites with that word in their Web address. Websitez searches domain names for the keywords you enter. If you enter the word *invest,* you will discover that there are several hundred sites with some form of the word in their domain names.

your search is that, even though all of the tools may index much of the same material, each tool has different internal criteria for ranking and different ways of presenting the results of a search. Thus, you may find dramatically different hits at the top of the list of different search engines. Try using the same keywords or phrases in several different tools to see how the results differ.

Choose Tools Suited to Your Subject

If you have a broad subject, a common topic, or are still curious in a more general sense and have not yet narrowed your topic to its final focus, use an index or directory. If you have a more specific search, such as a particular phrase, or an unusual topic, use a search engine. One indicator that may help you decide between directory and search engine would be the results you get from searching in one of the online encyclopedias. If the encyclopedia has an entry, the subject is probably general enough to locate in a directory; if there is no entry, you might choose the engine instead.

Many directories now have search engines connected with them, either as additional places to look or as part of their database. LookSmart (*www.looksmart.com*) is a good example of a directory that is also connected to a general search engine (AltaVista).

Use a topic-specific tool if there is one in the subject area you are investigating. Some examples of these tools would be Medline (*igm.nlm.nih.gov*) for medicine, FindLaw (*www.findlaw.com*) for law, FedStats (*www.fedstats.gov*) for statistics kept by the federal government, or SciCentral (*www.scicentral.com*) for links to science sites. Topic-specific tools, whether directories, engines, or combinations, often provide the most efficient way to find plentiful information in otherwise highly-specific topic areas.

Use a regional tool if your focus has geographical or cultural boundaries. If, for example, you want information about crocodiles in Australia and you want the information from Australia, choose one of

Search Tip

As a rule of thumb, try to phrase your searches so that the engine returns 200 or fewer relevant hits. (If you do a multiple keyword search, as discussed on page 50, you might see thousands of returned hits, but still be well within the 200 relevant hits near the beginning.) With just a little practice, you should be able to go through about 200 hits in an hour. That means looking through the list, reading the titles and descriptions, and clicking on the promising ones (and then saving, printing, or recording the URL or the Australian search tools, such as Web Wombat (*www.intercom.com.au/wombat/*) or Yahoo Australia and New Zealand (*www. yahoo.com.au*).

Remember, too, that the Web has resources other than written information: there are names, addresses, and phone numbers of people and companies. If what you need is a telephone interview or a corporate brochure, use one of the tools for finding names and addresses. These include InfoSpace (*www.infospace.com*) and various telephone directories like the GTE SuperPages (*superpages.gte.net*). Similarly, there are pictures, sounds, software, and so on. For a picture, try the "Picture This" feature from Lycos (*www.lycos.com*) or "Isurf" from Yahoo (*www.yahoo.com*).

Search Logic

There is a story about an old woodcutter who brought a chain saw back to the store for a refund. "You told me that with this saw I could cut down a hundred trees in a morning," he said. "But I can barely get one small tree cut down after working hard all day." The storekeeper took the saw, looked it over, and then pulled the starting cord. The saw immediately started up with a roar. Staring at the saw with amazement, the old woodcutter asked, "What's that noise?"

The point of this story is that any tool will work much better if you know how to use it. Search tools on the Internet are the same. By learning a little about how they work and how they can be controlled, you will be able to search powerfully and effectively.

Single-Word Searches

For specific or highly unusual words, such as

Search Tip

Create a file or draw a grid on a piece of paper that will help you organize the items you find in your search activity. Provide a column for each of the following: the search tool used, keywords or expressions used, results (in number of hits and usefulness, or how far you got in looking through them), the date of the activity, and comments. Later you may find it difficult to remember if you used a particular phrase in a particular tool. A reference sheet can save you from covering the same ground over again.

Search Tip

Use a directory to narrow down your topic area to a more specific subtopic and then perform a keyword search only within that subtopic area.

those found in science or the more esoteric arenas of learning, single-word searches can be excellent. For example, if you need information on the cosmetic preservative methylchloroisothiazolinone, you can simply type that chemical name into a search engine by itself. AltaVista returns about 120 hits, a good number to provide you with adequate selectivity. The botanical species name of a plant (benjamina), the chemical name of a refrigerant (dichlorodifluoromethane), or the Greek name of a rhetorical trope (epizeuxis) would be other examples.

Multiple-Word Searches

For more common words or more general words, however, a single-word search will usually yield too many hits to process. Suppose you want to find out about the printing of books and engravings in the Renaissance. If you search for *printing* in AltaVista, you will get more than three million hits. Similarly, *Renaissance* yields about eight hundred thousand hits. One remedy to this overabundance is that you can enter several words at the same time into a search engine. You could therefore type in the words *Renaissance printing* together. When you type a single word or multiple words (separated by spaces) into a search engine, most of the engines interpret this as a keyword search. This kind of search will find all pages that contain any of the words you have specified. Moreover, the search will find the words in any order and in any location in the document.

For example, suppose you are looking for information about the formulas in shampoo. If you perform a keyword search using the phrase *consumer product chemistry,* the engine will return every page that mentions any one of these three words anywhere on the page. Thus, you will see pages about

Search Tip

E-directory lists many regional search engines around the world (*www.edirectory.com*).

Search Tip

Even though the engines interpret the search words in a spaced list to be a keyword search meaning "either this one or that one, or that one, or maybe more than one," and even though a keyword search of several terms will return a seemingly daunting number of hits, they are ranked according to how many of the terms are found and how close together they are. Provide a very specific search by simply typing in a long list of words. Thus, a query for *west coast surfboard manufacturing sixties fiberglass* will generate thousands of hits, but the first ones in the list will be highly relevant to all the words.

"Consumer Protest over Dangerous Toys," "New Products Announced by Honda," "Sale on Chemistry Sets," and so forth.

Therefore, typing in the *Renaissance printing* expression means, "Give me every page containing the word *Renaissance,* the word *printing,* or both, in any order, anywhere in the document."

Boolean Operators

But what if you want to control how the words are searched for, and in our printing example, receive only hits that contain both *Renaissance* and *printing*? Interestingly enough, the solution to this problem was provided in the nineteenth century by English mathematician, George Boole, who invented a small set of logical operators that help searchers refine their queries to yield a manageable number of hits. The original Boolean operators are AND, OR, and NOT.

AND. In a Boolean AND search, such as *hardwood AND inlay,* both terms must be in the document in order for a match to be made and thus the return of a hit by the search engine. If a particular page mentions only *hardwood* or only *inlay,* no match will be made. Therefore AND is a restrictor—it narrows down the number of hits. Example: *drain AND pipe.*

OR. In a Boolean OR search, a match will be made and a hit returned if one, the other, or both terms are found on the page. Thus, OR is an expander—it increases the number of hits. Example: *bicycle OR tricycle.*

NOT. In a Boolean NOT search (sometimes used as AND NOT), pages containing the term after the NOT are excluded from the returned hits. Thus, NOT is also a restrictor. Example: *wine NOT champagne* will return pages with the word *wine* on them but not pages with the word *champagne* on them. Caution: Use NOT carefully, because you might otherwise exclude pages you really want to see. In the example just cited, a page titled, "Wine and Champagne Information" would be excluded, and you would miss all the information about wine on it. NOT can

Search Tip

If you want to use Boolean expressions, and especially NOT operators, read the "Help" section of the search engine you want to use to see whether Boolean is supported, either in the basic search mode or in an advanced mode. Also check to see whether the engine uses NOT or AND NOT for its NOT search. (For example, AltaVista and Excite use AND NOT, while Lycos and HotBot use NOT.)

be quite useful for eliminating unwanted hits that were returned amid wanted ones. For example, if you search for *watercraft,* you will find many hits referring to sailboats. But if you are interested only in jet ski equipment and canoes, you might restrict your search by eliminating terms you do not want: *watercraft AND NOT sail AND NOT boat* reduces the number of hits by more than eighty percent.

Let's see what these operators can do for the search about printing in the Renaissance. Since we want to restrict our hits from the millions, we will use the AND operator. A search using *Renaissance AND printing* yields 18,000 hits with the AltaVista search engine. That's much better than several million, but still high. Fortunately, Boolean operators can be combined, and we can further narrow our search by adding some refining words. A search for *Renaissance AND printing AND law* yields something over 5,000 hits. However, the hits are now focusing on law, rather than printing in general.

Boolean Logic Improved

Some search engines support an additional operator, NEAR. The NEAR operator in AltaVista, for example, locates two terms that occur within ten words of each other. When words are in close proximity to each other, there is an increased likelihood that the terms are related to a single concept. A search for *Renaissance NEAR printing* yields 850 hits, much closer to our ideal of fewer than 200. And even with 800, the search engines use ranking algorithms, based on how frequently the terms occur and how close together they are, so that the first hits in the list are likely to be the most useful.

Some search engines also support nesting, which allows you to create more complex Boolean searches, as in *childbirth AND (natural OR "at home").* Nesting is useful for performing automatic trimming of results at the same time you are specifying several synonyms for part of the search string.

Search Tip

If you really like to use Boolean operators, try Lycos, which, in addition to the ones mentioned, supports ADJ (adjacent), OADJ (ordered adjacent), FAR, ONEAR (ordered NEAR), and BEFORE.

Limits of Boolean Logic

The AND search and even the NEAR search do not guarantee that the actual topic made up of the words searched for will be found.

Suppose, for example, that you search for *Renaissance NEAR printing.* Suppose also that the search engine you are using has indexed a page devoted to miscellaneous items of historical interest, and that these sentences are on the page: "This was the state of medicine in the Renaissance. Now let us turn to printing in the nineteenth century." As you can see, the words *Renaissance* and *printing* do occur NEAR each other, thus yielding a legitimate hit, and yet this page has nothing to do with printing in the Renaissance.

Exact Phrase Searches

What we really want, you'll say, are the exact words *"Renaissance printing."* When the words are together, in that order, we are more likely to get just what we want. Enter the exact phrase search. Many search engines allow just this kind of search by surrounding the words with quotation marks. Notice the dramatic difference these marks make: In AltaVista the two words (with no quotation marks) *Renaissance printing* yield 855,000 hits. But surrounding them with quotation marks for an exact phrase search reduces the hits to about 70. Suddenly, the search becomes intensely focused and manageable. Some engines allow you to use another new Boolean operator ADJ (meaning "adjacent to"), which will return all pages where the words are next to each other, similar to an exact phrase search except that two words can be in either order. For example, a search on *fence ADJ slat* would return all pages with the phrases *fence slat* or *slat fence.*

Creativity in Searching

But, you now object, what if there is a discussion about Renaissance printing that doesn't use that exact phrase? One of the keys to successful searching is the ability to generate multiple synonyms, synonymous phrases, and alternative ways your subject might be expressed. (If you followed the advice at the beginning of this chapter, you will have a handy list already.) How else could our topic be phrased? An exact phrase search on *"Printing in the Renaissance"* yields five more hits. *"Renaissance book publishing"* yields another hit.

Wild Cards or Truncation Searches

Another powerful tool for the researcher is the ability to search for part of a word, matching all forms of the word. For our printing search, we might think, "What if there is a document out there that discusses printers but doesn't use the word *printing?* Rather than perform separate searches on every form of the word *print,* we can use a wild card search. In many search engines, the wild card is an asterisk. Thus, if we search for the exact phrase (using quotation marks) *"Renaissance print*"* the engine will return every page with the word *Renaissance* followed by either *print, prints, printers, printing,* or *printed.* In fact, such a search in AltaVista returns over 200 hits.

Plus and Minus Operators

Some engines allow the use of plus (+) and minus (–) operators, which function similarly to Boolean AND and NOT. The plus means "must include" and the minus means "must not include." A word with neither plus nor minus before it means "preferred but not essential." The search *+epic Homer –Latin* would thus tell the engine that the word *epic* must be included, *Homer* is preferred to be included, and *Latin* must not be included. Note that there is no space between the plus or minus operator and the term, but there is a space before the operator: *+speaker +stereo +"acoustic suspension"* (note that you can perform "must include" or "must not include" on an exact phrase).

Capitalizing Names

Two words together beginning with capital letters are assumed by many engines to be a proper name or title. A search for *Samuel Johnson* will thus look for the capitalized name of the eighteenth century writer, Samuel Johnson.

Concept Search

Some search engines (such as Excite) are intelligent in the sense that they recognize that certain words are related to general concepts. For example, if you search for the phrase *rain showers,* you will get all pages referring to weather in general if the engine is performing a concept search, since rain is related to the concept of weather. It is sometimes difficult to understand what the computer is "thinking" about when you see the results of a concept search, because you may find pages returned that seem to have nothing to do with your search terms. Nevertheless, occasionally a concept search can be quite helpful.

Pipes

The Infoseek search engine allows searchers to create and search subsets by using pipes. A pipe is a logical operator indicated by the vertical bar | symbol. For example, the search command *aircraft |*

cost | parts | bolts will extract from the database all references to air-craft, then from those hits extract all references to cost, from those hits all references to parts, and finally from those hits all references to bolts.

Conducting Your Search

Here are some suggestions for improving the results of your searches.

1. List search terms in the order of importance. For a keyword search, enter several words (at least two and as many as seven or eight), listing the most important words first. The order of search terms makes a difference in result reporting. For example, suppose we are researching urban legends, and we want to find out what is behind the story that, after a private drink with a strange woman, some young men are awakening in ice-filled bath tubs with a kidney missing. Searching AltaVista for *kidney ice bath emergency stolen tub* does not present any relevant hits near the top of the list. But rearranging the order of keywords to *stolen kidney ice bath emergency tub* gives us the information we want. (Note: in this case, better strategy would be to use the truncation *kidney** to find both singular and plural forms. And perhaps an exact phrase search for *"stolen kidney*"* would be very useful as well.)

2. Add and subtract search terms. Think of searching as an excursion into the wilderness of information. As you head toward the peak of enlightenment, you may have to alter your path a bit if a large boulder gets in the way. Enter your search terms and look at the hits you get. If the first twenty hits do not produce the information you want, add some new words to your current search list, rearrange the order of the words,

Search Tip

If you follow the advice stated earlier about using multiple-search tools, you can get a good feel about how different engines respond to the same set of keywords. In our kidney example, for instance, the original search string *kidney ice bath emergency stolen tub* in HotBot produces highly relevant results at the top of the reported hits, while AltaVista does not. Remember, search tools differ. Use that fact to your advantage.

Search Tip

If you are searching for a name or term that is commonly misspelled, first be certain that you are using the correct spelling. Additionally, you might also enter the common misspelling, just in case the word has been misspelled by someone else. For example: *dinosaur raptor rapter.*

or subtract some terms. This is a particularly effective way to use the Boolean NOT or the minus operator.

For example, suppose you want to add an electric spa to a house. The label on the spa says, "Requires 50 amp circuit." The problem is that you don't know what wire size to use for a new 50 amp circuit. So you go to AltaVista and type in the following: *wire size 50 amp load voltage drop*. AltaVista registers four million hits, and the first bunch all seem to cover various types of amplifier (for which the word *amp* is a shortened form). So, you decide to subtract *amp* and revise the search string to: *wire size 50 load voltage drop –amp** the last of which subtracts all pages that have *amp* or *amps* on them. This gives 1.6 million matches, but the second one is a wire size calculator. So, on this refined search, you have found your answer within the first ten hits.

3. Use synonymous phrases that move up or down a level of generalization. When you construct a list of synonymous words and phrases related to your key concepts, vary the level of generalization you use, so that some words are more specific than the key concepts and some are more general. For example, suppose your subject is growing apples. You perform exact phrase searches under *"apple growing,"* and *"growing apples"* but find a few items relevant to your interest. What other possible phrases might be used in an article that would cover this topic? You might search on broader phrases like *"fruit tree farming," "fruit orchards,"* or even *"farming and food production,"* or you might search on narrower phrases like *"Washington Red Delicious"* or *"apple juice."* If you perform a keyword search, you might even mix levels of generalization and search for *apple growing trees fruit farming juice Gala Fuji* to see what results you get.

4. Surf backwards. One of the great values of the Web and the ability to link pages to each other is that site creators often link their pages to other pages with similar content. If you find, say, a site about colorful tree frogs, you will notice that the site creator most likely has a set of hyperlinks to other such sites. By clicking on these, you can surf over to them. However, in addition to the sites linked from this page, you can also locate sites liked to the page by other creators. In other words, just as this site creator has found other sites to put on this page, some other sites somewhere have found this page useful enough to put its link on those pages. To find these other sites, you can use the link: "field search" in AltaVista or the "links to this URL" in HotBot. The query *link:www.pets.com* will find all the sites that list that hyperlink on their pages.

5. Guess a location. The address or URL (Uniform Resource Locator) of a Web site is, surprisingly, often guessable. Many companies use a standard form of URL, which is www.*company*.com, where *company* is the name of the company. Thus, for example, Sony is found at *www.sony.com* and you can figure out how to get to Disney, Honda, and NBC the same way. Companies with long names often abbreviate them in some guessable way, as for example *www.nytimes.com* is the *New York Times,* and the URL with *adage* in the middle will bring up *Advertising Age* and with *popsci* in the middle will get you *Popular Science.*

Moreover, that middle word is often the key to a site's content even when not identifying a famous company. The formula, www.*subject*.com is also a useful one to try. What, for example, do you think you would find at *www.fraud.com* or *www.weather.com?* Try the standard form with *salami* or *search* or *chocolate* or *toys* or *urbanlegends* and see what happens.

Along similar lines, you can get to the home page of most state governments by typing in www.state.*pz*.us, where *pz* is the two-letter postal abbreviation for the state, as in *ca* for California or *tx* for Texas.

6. Search URLs. A somewhat unusual but often effective search strategy is to search just the content of actual Web addresses, the URLs. AltaVista, HotBot, and InfoSeek all offer this function. Suppose, for example, you are interested in some articles about investing. You can use the URL search to find all pages with the file name of *invest.html*. In AltaVista and InfoSeek, use the search command *url:invest.html* and in HotBot choose "links to this URL."

7. Check the article length. Some search engines list the length of each

Search Tip

Remember that .com is not the only top-level domain. When searching by subject, you might also try www.*subject*.org to find organizations.

hit in kilobytes, which allows you to know in advance whether the hit is long or short. A length of only one or two kilobytes is likely to be just a list of links or very short commentary, while a length of fifteen kilobytes is likely to have substantial discussion. If you are using an engine that does not report article length in advance, simply go to the page and use your browser's ability to report the length for you. In Netscape Navigator, use "View," then "Document Info." In Netscape Communicator, use "View" and then "Page Info," and in Internet Explorer, use "File," then "Properties."

Checking page length is important if you are thinking about printing or saving a document. Sometimes a hit will land you in the middle of a lengthy document, and if you are not careful, you may find yourself printing thirty or forty pages that you did not anticipate.

Search Tip

The *url:* function does not support truncation, so you must search on alternate forms manually: *investing.html, invest. htm, investing.htm.*

8. Search within a document. When you first bring up a document, you may wonder where exactly your keywords occur in it. To find out, use the "Edit," then "Find" function in Netscape or "Edit," then "Find (on this page)" in Internet Explorer and enter a word or phrase. The browser will search the displayed document for the string. Alternatively, you can save the document and later bring it up in your word processor for searching with "Edit," then "Find."

9. Back up to find out where you are. When you click on a hit from a search engine, you are connected directly to the page where the search terms were matched. It is not always clear exactly where you have arrived. You may see something like, "Chapter 5: The Triumph of Palladian Architecture." Who wrote this? What is the book about? To answer these questions, look at the URL (address) you have connected to. If may look something like this: *http://www.some.edu/faculty/jones/architec/ch5.htm.* The page you are reading is the lowest level of a series of directories beginning with the Web site (*www.some.edu*), dropping to a *faculty* directory, then to a *jones* directory, and so on. To learn more about the context of your chapter 5, first look for a "Back" or "Previous" or "Home" button, which will allow you to return to a higher level.

If you cannot find any return features, go to the right end of the URL and chop off the *ch5.htm* and then press the return button on your keyboard. This will sometimes yield an "access denied" message, but many times it will back you up one level in the hierarchy and you can see what the higher directory (*architec* in this case) contains. You might find a book title, author, or a useful file name such as *intro.html*. If you still need more information, chop off the *architec* directory and back up to *jones* to see what is there. Back up as far as you want or need to in order to find out the information you need about the work and its author.

10. **Read the search tips or help information at each tool.** Each search tool has its own methods for constructing search strings or for navigating through its directory levels. Many of the tools have "value added" features as well (such as Lycos's image searching), and you should get to know how these work by reading the help information. You will learn how to perform more sophisticated searches, how to restrict or expand searches, and how to use the site more efficiently.

Common Search Errors

Here is a list of the most common errors made by inexperienced users of search tools, beginning with the most common.

A Boolean Expression to Find an Exact Phrase

A searcher will sometimes connect the words of an exact phrase with Boolean AND operators, as in *used AND motorcycles, Jane AND Austen, historical AND map*. If you are looking for two or more words together in order, use quotation marks for an exact phrase search. Searching for *used AND motorcycles* yields 1.2 million hits with AltaVista, while searching for *"used motorcycles"* yields 1500.

Search Tip

Whenever you find a useful page, be sure that you save the URL and all pertinent information so that you can cite the source. If you print the page with your browser, the URL will be automatically printed with it. But if you save the file in your word processor, the address will not be included unless it is a specific part of the page. If you should forget to keep the URL but have a copy of the article, you can use a full-text search engine to locate the article. Find a four- or five-word phrase from the article that contains its most unusual words. Then perform an exact phrase search for these words. The engine will almost always take you right to the article. You should develop the habit of bookmarking each site you use so that you can return to it easily. See the section on p. 55 for more details.

A Single-Word Keyword Search

As mentioned earlier, if you are looking for a very specific, infrequently used word, such as toxoplasmosis or cirrhosis, a single-word keyword search can be quite effective. However, for many words, a single-word search will yield hundreds of thousands or even millions of hits, with little way to arrange them in a useful order. Try one of these terms in your favorite engine and see how many hits you get: *travel, sports, rivers, wrestling, nursing.* It is usually best to use from two to seven or eight words as a keyword search string rather than a single-word search.

Misspelled Word

A regular error in searching is the use of a misspelled word in a search string. Common examples include typographical errors (such as *action figurwes*), homonyms (*corn AND maze* instead of *maize, ham radio sights* instead of *sites*), and incorrect spellings (*fantacy, Bacon's Rebillion).* Type carefully and check your spelling.

Inappropriate Capitalization

Using lowercase letters will, in most search engines, find all occurrences of the word in either lowercase or capitals. However, using a capital letter will usually find only occurrences that are capitalized. Thus, instead of searching for *Ulcerative Colitis,* it would be more fruitful to search for *ulcerative colitis* (and better still to make it an exact phrase search: *"ulcerative colitis").*

Improper Use of Operators

One example of this is failure to put space before the plus or minus sign, as in *pizza+recipes* or *job+center.* Another is failure to close quotation marks or parentheses, as in *"lyme disease.* Last is the use of too much truncation with a wild card. If you want to find both *rat* and *rats,* you might think to search with the wild card *rat** which will indeed find both *rat* and *rats.* But it will also find every occurrence of *ratio, rational, rations, ratings, rattletrap,* and so on.

Search Tip

Wild cards are best used in combination with at least one other whole word to help circumscribe the search.

Saving and Printing

Once you have found a page of useful information, there are several ways to deal with the question of preserving it for use. Here are some considerations to help you determine which to choose in each case.

Bookmarking

If you have your own computer, or are using a personal bookmark file, you can simply add the page to your bookmarks so that you can return to it whenever you wish to read or copy text. The advantages of bookmarking are these: no disk storage space is required, and no paper is wasted. The disadvantages are these: you must have a computer and access to the Web to read the information, and the Web site with the information must be up and still have the information posted. (The Internet might be busy, the site might be down, or the site creator may have changed or dismounted the information.) If you like working exclusively on the computer, and if your research is such that an occasional delay will not be fatal, bookmarking can be a good choice.

Saving

You can save Web documents to disk in several ways. You can save the document as an HTML file, the existing hypertext markup language of the document itself. This allows you to bring the document up in your browser even if you are not on the Web at the time. Use the "File," "Open File" command and go to the folder where you have saved the document. If the document has a simple structure, you may be able to bring it directly into one of the powerful word processors like recent versions of Microsoft Word.

Alternatively, you can save the file as a plain text ASCII file, usually with a *.txt* extension. This type of file can be edited in even simple word processors. Once again, however, very complex pages may be converted with a high degree of unwanted formatting.

Lastly, you can cut and paste sections of the document (or the entire document) directly into your word processor. The best way to do this is to create a separate file for each cut-and-paste, and include a full bibliographic reference and the URL. (If you paste directly into a paper you are working on, remember to show clearly where

the text from the document begins and ends and to attach a bibliographic reference, or at least the URL, so that you do not accidentally steal and plagiarize the text.)

Printing

If you want to preserve the look of the original Web page, with all its layout and graphics, you can print it. The advantages of printing are these: you can read and work on your research away from the computer; you can highlight, make notes, and rearrange pages. The disadvantages are these: you will have to retype whatever quotations you use.

Be sure to check the file size before you print. Even scrolling through a file can sometimes produce a misleading idea about how long the file is.

Saving Graphics

To save a picture from a Web page, right click in Windows or hold down the mouse button with a Macintosh and you will get a menu that allows you to save the graphic. Be sure to give it the file extension that belongs to it (*.gif* or *.jpg*) so that you can easily identify it as a graphic later on.

Search Tip

Some Web pages are constructed so that they do not print out on a black and white printer. Especially problematic are black pages with white text. Attempting to print one of these on a laser printer will yield only a blank page. To capture text from a page like this, use cut and paste and put the text into a word processor or even Word

★ Chapter 5 ★

Evaluating Web Sources

―――➤●◄―――

"If students are to succeed, if their navigation is to lead them to safe harbor, then information-age schooling must go far beyond access, organization, and absorption. Fundamentally, and from the beginning, schooling must also emphasize critical analysis, integration, and application. . . . We must teach students to sort the fluff from the substance in the information they gather." –Daniel E. Kinnaman, News Editor, *Technology and Learning*

"The basic principle of commercial media–that content and advertising remain distinguishable–is being eroded in this digital age. . . . In the digital age, advertising is content–or at least it can be. . . . The best hopes for integrity in media–both new and old–are educated consumers able to judge for themselves what is and isn't appropriate and savvy marketers who know that you can't fool the public." –Dan Ruby, Editor in Chief, *New Media*

"The central work of life is interpretation." –Proverb

―――➤●◄―――

Preparing to Evaluate

The value of evaluation should be obvious to everyone who believes that there is a difference between a real steak and a piece of thickly sliced bologna. But those who are new to the finding and processing of information do not always recognize the wide range of forms and quality that information can have.

The Diversity of Information. Think about the magazine section in your local grocery store. If you reach out with your eyes closed and grab the first magazine you touch, you are about as likely to get a supermarket tabloid as you are a respected journal (actually more likely, since many respected journals don't fare well in grocery stores). Now imagine that your grocer is so accommodating that he lets anyone in town print up a magazine and put it in the magazine section. Now if you reach out blindly, you might get the *Elvis Lives with Aliens Gazette* just as easily as *Atlantic Monthly* or *Time.*

Welcome to the World Wide Web. As I hope my analogy makes clear, there is an extremely wide variety of material on the Web, equally wide-ranging in its accuracy, reliability, and value. Unlike most traditional information media (books, magazines, organizational documents), no one has to approve the content before it is made public. It is your job as a searcher, then, to evaluate what you locate in order to determine whether it suits your needs.

Information Exists on a Continuum of Reliability and Quality. Information is everywhere on the Web, existing in large quantities and continuously being created and revised. This information exists in a large variety of kinds (facts, opinions, stories, interpretations, statistics) and is created for many purposes (to inform, to persuade, to sell, to present a viewpoint, and to create or change an attitude or belief). For each of these various kinds and purposes, information exists on many levels of quality or reliability. It ranges from very good to very bad and includes every shade in between.

Evaluation Tip

Try to select sources that offer as much of the following information as possible:

✵ Author's name (note that the author may be a person or an organization)
✵ Author's title or position
✵ Author's organizational affiliation
✵ Date of page creation or version
✵ Author's contact information
✵ Some of the indicators of information quality (see p. 59)

Screening Information

Pre-evaluation. The first stage of evaluating your sources takes place before you do any searching. Take a minute to ask yourself what exactly you are looking for. Do you want facts, opinions (authoritative or just anyone's), reasoned arguments, statistics, narratives, eyewitness reports, descriptions? Is the purpose of your research to get new ideas, to find either factual or reasoned support for a position, to survey opinion, or something else? Once you decide on your purpose, you will be able to screen sources much more quickly by testing them against your research goal. If, for example, you are writing a research paper, and if you are looking for both facts and well-argued opinions to support or challenge a position, you will know which sources can be quickly passed by and which deserve a second look, simply by asking whether each source appears to offer facts and well-argued opinions, or just unsupported claims.

Select Sources Likely to Be Reliable. Becoming proficient at this will require experience, of course, but even a beginning researcher can take a few minutes to ask, "What source or what kind of source would be the most credible for providing information in this particular case?" Which sources are likely to be fair, objective, lacking hidden motives, showing quality control? It is important to keep these considerations in mind, so that you will not simply take the opinion of the first source or two you can locate. By thinking about these issues while searching, you will be able to identify suspicious or questionable sources more readily. With so many sources to choose from in a typical search, there is no reason to settle for unreliable material.

Evaluation Tip

Search engines deliver you to a specific page, as if you closed your eyes, grabbed a book or magazine, opened to a page and then opened your eyes. You often do not know whose site you are visiting. A good practice in this case is to visit the home page of the document you have found and find out about the person or organization producing the work. Is this likely to be a reliable source? Look for a button or link that will take you to a home or main page for the site.

The Tests of Information Quality

Reliable Information Is Power. You may have heard that "knowledge is power," or that information, the raw material of knowledge, is power. But the truth is that when you must act on it, only some information is power: reliable information. Information serves as the basis for beliefs, decisions, choices, and understanding our world. If we make a decision based on wrong or unreliable information, we do not have power–we have defeat. If we eat something harmful that we believe to be safe, we can become ill; if we avoid something good that we believe to be harmful, we have needlessly restricted the enjoyment of our lives. The same thing applies to every decision to travel, purchase, or act, and every attempt to understand.

Source Evaluation Is an Art. Source evaluation–the determination of information quality–is something of an art. That is, there is no single perfect indicator of reliability, truthfulness, or value. Instead, you must make an inference from a collection of clues or indicators, based on the use you plan to make of your source. If, for example, what you need is a reasoned argument, such as the merits of proposed campaign reform, then a source with a clear, well-argued position can stand on its own, without the need for a prestigious author to support it. On the other hand, if you need a judgment to support (or rebut) some position, such as the real risk of pesticide residues on fruit, then that judgment will be strengthened if it comes from a respected source. If you want reliable facts, such as traffic accident trends over the last twenty years, then using facts from a source that meets certain criteria of quality will help ensure the probability that those facts are indeed reliable.

The CARS Checklist

The CARS Checklist (Credibility, Accuracy, Reasonableness, Support) is designed for ease of use. Few sources will meet every criterion in the list, and even those that do may not possess the highest level of quality possible. But if you learn to use the criteria in this list, you will be much better able to separate the high-quality information from the poor-quality information.

Credibility

Because people have always made important decisions based on information, evidence of authenticity and reliability–or credibility, believability–has always been important. If you read an article saying that the area where you live will experience a major earthquake in the next six months, it is important that you should know whether or not to believe the information. Some questions to ask about general credibility might include these:

✫ Is there sufficient evidence presented to make the argument persuasive?
✫ Are there compelling arguments and reasons given?

⋆ Are there enough details for a reasonable conclusion about the information?

There are several tests you can apply to a source to help you judge how credible and useful it will be:

Author's Credentials. The author or source of the information should show some evidence of being knowledgeable, reliable, and truthful. Some questions you might ask would include the following:

⋆ What about this source makes it believable (or not)?
⋆ How does this source know this information?
⋆ Why should I believe this source over another?

As you can see, the key to credibility is the question of trust. Here are some clues to credibility:

⋆ Author's education, training, and/or experience in a field relevant to the information. Look for biographical information, the author's title, or position of employment
⋆ Author's contact information (e-mail or postal mail address, telephone number)
⋆ Organizational authorship from a known and respected organization (corporate, governmental, or non-profit)
⋆ Organizational authorship reflecting an appropriate area of expertise
⋆ Author's reputation or standing among peers

Evidence of Quality Control. Most scholarly journal articles pass through a peer review process, whereby several readers must examine and approve content before it is published. Statements issued in the name of an organization have almost always been seen and approved by several people. (But note the difference between, "Allan Thornton, employee of the National Oceanographic and Atmospheric Agency,

Evaluation Tip

Feel free to contact the author of a source by e-mail or telephone when such contact information is given. Many authors are willing to clarify points or explain details further. Communicating with the author will also give you more evidence about credibility.

says that a new ice age is near," and "The National Oceanographic and Atmospheric Agency said today that a new ice age is near." The employee is speaking for himself, whereas a statement in the name of NOAA represents the official position of NOAA.)

Evidence of quality control of Web material includes these items:

★ Information presented on corporate, government, or organizational Web sites
★ Online journals that use refereeing (peer review) by editors or others
★ Postings of information taken from books or journals that have a quality control process

Indicators of Lack of Credibility. You can sometimes tell by the tone, style, or competence of the writing whether or not the information is suspect. Here are a few clues to lack of credibility:

★ Anonymity
★ No indication of a third party editor or publisher to ensure the quality and reliability of the information
★ Negative metainformation. If all the reviews are critical, be careful. (See the discussion about metainformation later in this chapter.)
★ Bad grammar or misspelled words. Most educated people use grammar fairly well and check their work for spelling errors. An occasional split infinitive or comma in the wrong place is not unusual, but more than two or three spelling or grammar errors is cause for caution, at least. Whether the errors come from carelessness or ignorance, neither puts the information or the writer in a favorable light.

Evaluation Tip

The top-level domain *.gov* is used by state and federal government agencies and indicates that the information has the sanction of that government agency. Information from these domains is usually highly reliable. For example, you can obtain reliable census information from the Census Bureau at *www.census.gov* or information about medicine, food, or cosmetics from the Food and Drug Administration at *www.fda.gov*

Accuracy

The goal of the accuracy test is to ensure that the information is actually correct: up-to-date, factual, detailed, exact, and comprehensive. For example, even though a very credible writer said something that was correct twenty years ago, it may not be correct today. Similarly, a reputable source might be giving up-to-date information, but the information may be only partial and not give the full story. Here are some concepts related to accuracy:

Timeliness. Some work is timeless, like the classic novels and stories, or like the thought-provoking philosophical work of Aristotle and Plato. Other work has a limited useful life because of advances in the discipline (psychological theory, for example), and some work is outdated very quickly (like technology news). You must therefore be careful to note when the information you find was created, and then decide whether it is still of value (and how much value). You may need information within the past ten years, five years, or even two weeks. But old is not necessarily bad: nineteenth-century American history books or literary anthologies can be highly educational because they can function as comparisons with what is being written or anthologized now. In many cases, though, you want accurate, up-to-date information.

An important idea connected with timeliness is the dynamic, fluid nature of information and the fact that constant change means constant changes in timeliness. The facts we learn today may be timely now, but tomorrow will not be. Especially in technology, science, medicine, business, and other fields always in flux, we must remember to check and re-check our data from time to time, and realize that we will always need to update our facts.

Comprehensiveness. Any source that presents conclusions or that claims (explicitly or implicitly) to give a full and rounded story, should reflect the intentions of completeness and accuracy. In other words, the information should be comprehensive. Some writers argue that researchers should be sure that they have "complete" information before making a decision or coming to a conclusion. But with the advent of the information age, such a goal is impossible, if by "complete" we mean all possible information. No one can read 20,000 articles on the same subject before coming to a conclusion or making a decision. On the other hand, an information

Evaluation Tip

You can use your browser to find out when a Web page was last modified, even though there may not be a visible date on the page itself. In Netscape, use "View," "Page Info" and you will see a "Last Modified" field with a date. In Internet Explorer, using "File," "Properties" you will get the date the information was transferred to your disc, *not* the date the page was modified.

source that deliberately leaves out important facts, qualifications, consequences, or alternatives may be misleading or even intentionally deceptive. And since no single piece of information will offer the truly complete story, even if accuracy and fairness are intended, we must rely on more than one source to provide us with a fuller view of the situation.

Audience and Purpose. For whom is this source intended and for what purpose? If, for example, you find an article, "How Plants Grow," and children are the intended audience, then the material may be too simplified for your college botany paper. More important to the evaluation of information is the purpose for which the information was created. For example, an article titled, "Should You Buy or Lease a Car?" might have been written with the purpose of being an objective analysis, but it may instead have been written with the intention of persuading you that leasing a car is better than buying. In such a case, the information will most likely be highly biased or distorted. Such information is not useless, but the bias must be taken into consideration when interpreting and using the information. (In some cases, you may be able to find the truth by using only biased sources, some biased in one direction and some biased in the other.) Be sure, then, that the intended audience and purpose of the article are appropriate to your requirements or at least clearly in evidence so that you may take them into account. *Information pretending to objectivity but possessing a hidden agenda of persuasion or a hidden bias is quite common in our culture.*

Indicators of a Lack of Accuracy. In addition to an obvious tone or style that reveals a carelessness with detail or accuracy, there are several indicators that may mean the source is inaccurate, either in whole or in part:

- ★ No date on the document
- ★ Assertions that are vague or otherwise lacking detail
- ★ Sweeping rather than qualified language (that is, the use of *always, never, every, completely* rather than *usually, seldom, sometimes, tends,* and so forth)
- ★ An old date on information known to change rapidly
- ★ Very one-sided view that does not acknowledge opposing views or respond to them

Reasonableness

The test of reasonableness involves examining the information for fairness, objectivity, moderateness, and consistency.

Fairness. Fairness includes offering a balanced, reasoned argument, not selected or slanted. Even ideas or claims made by the source's opponents should be presented in an accurate manner. Pretending that the opponent has wild, irrational ideas or arguments no one could accept is to commit the straw man fallacy. A good information source will also possess a calm, reasoned tone, arguing or presenting material thoughtfully and without attempting to get you emotionally worked up. Pay attention to the tone and be cautious of highly emotional writing. Angry, hateful, critical, spiteful tones often betray an irrational and unfair attack under way rather than a reasoned argument. And writing that attempts to inflame your feelings to prevent you from thinking clearly is also unfair and manipulative.

Objectivity. There is no such thing as pure objectivity, but a good writer should be able to control his or her biases. Be aware that some organizations are naturally not neutral. For example, a professional antibusiness group will find, say, that some company or industry is overcharging for widgets. The industry trade association, on the other hand, can be expected to find that no such overcharging is taking place. Be on the lookout for slanted, biased, politically distorted work.

One of the biggest hindrances to objectivity is conflict of interest. Sometimes an information source will benefit in some way (usually financially, but sometimes politically or even emotionally or psychologically) if that source can get you to accept certain information rather than the pure and objective truth. For example, many sites that sell "natural" products (cosmetics, vitamins, clothes, food) often criticize their competitors for selling bad, unhealthy, or dangerous products. The criticism may be just, but because the messenger will gain financially if you believe the message, you should be very careful—and check somewhere else before spending money or believing the tale.

Moderateness. Moderateness is a test of

Evaluation Tip

Many Web sites are sponsored by news organizations that have printed or broadcast counterparts. As a general rule, if the printed or broadcast source is reliable, so too is the online counterpart. The online sites for *Time, CNN,* The *New York Times, ABC News,* and so forth, have the same reputation to uphold and the same resources to devote to fact checking and accuracy as their traditional media versions, and should therefore be just as professional. There have been a few notable exceptions, but those have indeed been exceptions. (Similarly, the online versions of the incredible sources, such as some of the tabloids, should be viewed with the same suspicion used for the printed version.)

the information against how the world really is. Use your knowledge and experience to ask if the information is really likely, possible, or probable. Most truths are ordinary. If a claim being made is surprising or hard to believe, use caution and demand more evidence than you might require for a lesser claim. Claims that seem to run against established natural laws also require more evidence. In other words, do a reality check. Is the information believable? Does it make sense? Or do the claims lack face validity? That is, do they seem to conflict with what you already know in your experience, or do they seem too exaggerated to be true? For example, does the statement, "Half of all Americans have had their cars stolen," pass the face validity test? Have half of your friends had their cars stolen? Is the subject on the news regularly (as we might assume it would be if such a level of theft were the case)?

It is important, of course, to remember that some truths are spectacular and immoderate. If you have read about, say, the Tulipmania in Holland in 1636–1637, where some single tulip bulbs sold for the equivalent of tens of thousands of dollars each, the idea of immoderate truth will not be so strange to you. Do not, therefore, automatically reject a claim or source simply because it is astonishing. Just be extra careful about checking it out.

Consistency. The consistency test simply requires that the argument or information does not contradict itself. Sometimes when people spin falsehoods or distort the truth, inconsistencies or even contradictions show up. These are evidence of unreasonableness. Perhaps an obvious example comes from some of the chain letters that circulate on the Internet and by fax machine: they affirm that they have come to you "to bring you cheer and good luck," only to threaten you (not very indirectly) with unemployment or death if you do not continue to circulate the letter.

World View. A writer's view of the world (political, economic, religious—including antireligious—and philosophical) often influences his or her writing profoundly, from the subjects chosen to the slant, the issues raised, issues ignored, fairness to opponents, kinds of examples, and so forth. Some writers' value systems permit them to fabricate evidence, lie, or falsify the positions of others for the sake of what they think is a noble cause—or perhaps political expediency. For these writers, political agendas take precedence over truth. Knowing about such distorting world views can therefore provide another evaluative test for reasonableness.

Indicators of a Lack of Reasonableness. Writers who put themselves in the way of the argument, either emotionally or because of self-interest, often reveal their lack of reasonableness. If, for example, you find a writer reviewing a book he opposes by asserting that "the entire book is completely worthless claptrap," you might suspect there is more than a reasoned disagreement at work. Here are some clues to a lack of reasonableness:

- ★ Intemperate tone or language ("stupid jerks," "shrill cries of my extremist opponents")
- ★ Overclaims ("Thousands of children are murdered every day in the United States.")
- ★ Sweeping statements of excessive significance ("This is the most important idea ever conceived!")
- ★ Conflict of interest ("Welcome to the Old Stogie Tobacco Company Home Page. To read our report, 'Cigarettes Make You Live Longer,' click here." or "When you buy a stereo, beware of other brands that lack our patented circuitry.")

Support

The area of support is concerned with the source and corroboration of the information. Much information, especially statistics and claims of fact, comes from other sources. Citing sources strengthens the credibility of the information. (Remember this when you write a research paper.)

Source Documentation or Bibliography. When facts or statistics are quoted, look to see whether their source is revealed, so that you could check their accuracy. Some source considerations include these:

- ★ Where did this information come from?
- ★ What sources did the information creator use?
- ★ Are the sources listed?
- ★ Is there a bibliography or other documentation?
- ★ Does the author provide contact information in case you wish to discuss an issue or request further clarification?
- ★ What kind of support for the information is given?
- ★ How does the writer know this?

It is especially important for statistics to be documented. Otherwise, someone may be just making up numbers. Note that some information from corporate sites consists of descriptions of products, techniques, technologies, or processes with which the corporation is involved. If you are careful to distinguish between facts ("We mix X and Y together to get Z") and advertising ("This protocol is the best in the industry"), then such descriptions should be reliable.

Corroboration. See if other sources support this source.

Corroboration or confirmability is an important test of truth. And even in areas of judgment or opinion, if an argument is sound, there will probably be a number of people who adhere to it or who are in some general agreement with parts of it. Whether you're looking for a fact (like the lyrics to a song or the date of an event), an opinion (such as whether paper or plastic is the more environmentally friendly choice), or some advice (such as how to grow bromeliads), it is a good idea to triangulate your findings: that is, find at least three sources that agree. If the sources do not agree, do further research to find out the range of opinion or disagreement before you draw your conclusions.

Evaluation Tip

A quirk of human nature causes most of us to value what is scarce. Some information producers who want to manipulate us therefore pretend to have "secret" or "exclusive" information—which, of course, cannot therefore be corroborated. Be very careful of such information. Remember that, when it comes to information, "secret" is nearly a synonym for "gossip," and "exclusive" means roughly "unsubstantiated" or "unconfirmed."

What you are doing with corroboration, then, is using information to test information. Use one source, fact, point of view, or interpretation to test another. Find other information to support and reconfirm (or to challenge or rebut) information you have found. It is critical, of course, to consider the quality of the corroborative information. There is at least one situation on the Web now where more than a dozen "natural care" sites have all repeated the same false story that the surfactant sodium laureth sulfate (used in many cosmetics) causes cancer. (The owners of these sites sell products that do not contain this ingredient.) Finding the same claim on several of these sites is certainly not corroboration. For a corroborative test, you should look to disinterested third parties, in this case to the federal government, toxicology reports, and the like.

Corroboration is especially important when you find dramatic or surprising information (information failing the moderateness test, above). For example, a claim like the one just mentioned, that some commonly used substance is harmful, should be viewed with skepticism until it can be confirmed (or rebutted) by further research and by truly reliable sources. The claim may be true, but it seems unlikely that both government and consumer organizations would let a harmful chemical or other product go unchallenged.

External Consistency. While the test of corroboration involves finding out whether other sources contain the same new information as the source being evaluated, the test of external consistency compares what is familiar in the new source with what is familiar in other sources. That is, information is usually a mixture of old and new, of some things you already know and some things you do not. The test of external consistency asks, Where this source discusses facts or ideas I already know something about, does the source agree or harmonize or does it conflict, exaggerate, or distort? The reasoning is that if a source is faulty where it discusses something you already know, it is likely to be faulty in areas where you do not yet know, and you should therefore be cautious and skeptical about trusting it.

Indicators of a Lack of Support As you can readily guess, the lack of supporting evidence provides the best indication that there is indeed no available support. Be careful, then, when a source shows problems like these:

  ✵ Numbers or statistics presented without an identified source for them
  ✵ Absence of source documentation when the discussion clearly needs such documentation
  ✵ Lack of any other sources that present the same information or acknowledge that the same information exists (lack of corroboration)

Evaluation Tip

As you continue to work in the world of information, you should begin to develop an effective "baloney detector," which will enable you to sense when a claim is too good, too bad, too excessive, or too weird to be true. Suppose, for example, you receive a chain letter e-mail claiming that you will be paid five thousand dollars if you forward it to all your friends. How likely is that to be true? And if it were true, wouldn't you expect to hear about such an amazing deal on the nightly news or in the paper? You can keep your baloney detector tuned up by reading widely and getting a good sense of what generally happens, and what truths and myths are spreading around the Web or another part of the information environment.

Summary of the CARS Checklist for Research Source Evaluation

Credibility	Trustworthy source, the quality of evidence and argument, author's credentials, evidence of quality control, known or respected authority, organizational support. Goal: an authoritative source; a source that supplies some good evidence that allows you to trust it.
Accuracy	Up-to-date, factual, detailed, exact, comprehensive, audience and purpose reflect intentions of completeness and accuracy. Goal: a source that is correct today (not yesterday); a source that gives the whole truth.
Reasonableness	Fair, balanced, objective, reasoned, no conflict of interest, absence of fallacies or slanted tone. Goal: a source that engages the subject thoughtfully and reasonably; a source concerned with the truth.
Support	Listed sources, contact information, available corroboration, claims supported, documentation supplied. Goal: a source that provides convincing evidence for the claims made; a source you can triangulate (find at least two other sources that support it).

Living with Information: The CAFÉ Advice

Here is one last piece of advice to help you live well in the world of information: Take your information to the Café (Challenge, Adapt, File, Evaluate).

Challenge. Challenge information and demand accountability. Stand right up to the information and ask questions. How good is the evidence? Who says so? Why do they say so? Why was this information created? Why should I believe it? Why should I trust this source? How is it known to be true? Is it the whole truth? Is the argument reasonable? Who supports it?

Adapt. Adapt your skepticism and requirements for quality to fit the importance of the information and what is being claimed. Require more credibility and evidence for stronger claims. You are right to be a little skeptical of dramatic information or information that conflicts with commonly accepted ideas. The new information may be true, but you should require a robust amount of evidence from highly credible sources.

File. File new information in your mind rather than immediately believing or disbelieving it. Avoid premature closure. Do not jump to a conclusion or come to a decision too quickly. It is fine simply to remember that someone claims XYZ to be the case. You need not worry about believing or disbelieving the claim right away. Wait until more information comes in, you have time to think about the issue, and you gain more general knowledge.

Evaluate. Evaluate and reevaluate regularly. New information or changing circumstances will affect the accuracy and hence your evaluation of previous information. Recognize the dynamic, fluid nature of information. The saying, "Change is the only constant," applies to much information, especially in technology, science, medicine, and business.

Using Metainformation

Metainformation is information about information. Information workers all over the world are constantly poring over, processing, and evaluating information—and making notes. As the challenges produced by the increasing quantity of information continue, access to high quality metainformation will become increasingly important. Metainformation can take many forms, but there are two basic types, summary and evaluative.

Summary Metainformation

Summary metainformation includes all the shortened forms of information, such as abstracts, content summaries, indexes, tables of contents, compendiums, extracts, listings by subject or category, keywords, subject headings, best-seller lists, bibliographies, quotations, directories, and catalogs. This type of metainformation gives us a quick glance at what a work is about and allows us to consider many different sources without having to go through them completely.

Most Web search engines and directories provide a range of metainformation about the links they display in the hit lists, including a summary or the first few dozen words of the document, the document date, and the document size. The summary material provides a useful elaboration on titles that may not clearly indicate the nature of the site.

Evaluative Metainformation

Evaluative metainformation includes all the types that provide some judgment or analysis of content. This type includes reviews, recommendations, ratings, rankings, analyses, critiques, commentaries, awards, prizes, reputation among peers, responses, and opinions of reliability from a respected source.

Many search engines provide relevancy ratings of the hits they return, so that the searcher can see how closely together and how often the keywords occur in the given document. Directories often provide ratings (such as one to five stars or check marks) to indicate some measure of site value.

Summary and evaluative metainformation can be combined, resulting in the best form of metainformation, providing us with a quick overview and some evaluation of the value of the information. An example site would be StudyWeb (*www.studyweb.com*), an education-site directory that describes each site briefly and rates it for visual content and grade level.

Issues in the Use of Metainformation

Using the ratings or recommendations of others can be a powerful shortcut for many searches. The degree of reliance that is justified, however, depends on whether the criteria used to make the recommendation match the criteria you have in mind for a useful site. Some sites offer no explanation at all of their selection criteria, while some mention vaguely that the creators "spent months to compile" the listings or that the listings are "editors' picks." A few are a little more forthcoming. The creators of the Excite recommendations say that their recommended sites "have broad relevance in a single subject area . . . and demonstrate depth of content, excellent organization, and timeliness." Similarly, the creators of the Lycos Top 5% rate each selected site on the basis of content ("how informative a site is"), design ("layout and presentation"), and overall (which includes "amusement, personality, and charm"). The Scout Report

Evaluation Tip

You can determine how popular or useful other people think a site is by discovering how many other Web pages link to the site. A site with many links to it is probably held in high esteem by Web users. Use the *link:* command in AltaVista or InfoSeek (as in *link:www.pbs.com*) and you will see the number of other pages with that link on them. (As with any evaluation method, the link check is not always a good indicator. One notorious adult site has more than 14,000 links to it.)

Signpost creators say they are "looking for the most valuable and authoritative" sites–perhaps the clearest description of a criterion of reliability.

While the vagaries of selection criteria should be reason for caution in relying unthinkingly on recommended sites, the truth is that many of the recommended sites are in fact quite good. Even sites selected merely on the basis of popularity (as they are at 100hot.com) are often very useful. An emerging information technology concept is that of collaborative filtering, whereby many people's decisions (visiting sites, buying books, etc.) create rankings that others can use to help make decisions. There are some dangers with this method (see chapter 7 on critical thinking), but it has its uses as well. Most Web users are interested in quality information, and their choices are frequently helpful.

Metainformation Sites

Here are some sites that will show the variety of metainformation available on the Web:

Magellan Reviewed Sites
www.mckinley.com

Lycos Top 5%
point.lycos.com

Excite Reviews
www.excite.com

100Hot.Com
www.100hot.com

1001 Best Web Sites
www.zdnet.com/pccomp/webmap/

Scout Report Signpost
www.signpost.org/signpost/index.html

Web Assurance Bureau
www.wabureau.com

Web Associates Top 10
wwwa.com/awards.htm

Recreational Software Advisory Council
www.rsac.org

★ Chapter 6 ★

Using and Citing the Web as an Information Source

———➤●◄———

When you use the Web as a resource during your search for information, you should be aware of some issues relating to time management, privacy, and safety arising out of the nature of the Web itself. This chapter also includes information about how to cite the sources you locate.

———➤●◄———

Time and Quality Issues

Time Management

The fact that Web information comes quickly, without your having to get up and walk around a library creates the expectation that all information should arrive immediately. Hence, when it doesn't, there is often a feeling of impatience when using the Web. Some beginning Web searchers hastily conclude that "there is nothing on the Internet" after looking for five minutes. More seasoned searchers realize that they are really looking into a sea of millions of documents and images, and that finding a great collection of resources is often a time-consuming enterprise. A carefully planned search strategy and an adequate amount of allocated time will produce the best results. Searching impatiently or searching in stolen scraps of time here and there will lead only to frustration.

The time management issue has another, opposite side as well: Web addiction. Some users become so obsessed with surfing the Web that they lose track of time and spend far too many hours lost in cyberspace, often moving around without direction or purpose. Good advice is to plan your search time, allocating a certain amount depending on your schedule. When you do get on the Web, you do not need to spend every minute engaged in serious research; you can indeed plan some time simply to surf–to wander from one interesting site to another, following the links on various pages. Just be wary of the temptation to sit down at the computer after dinner for a "few minutes" of browsing, only to look up at the clock and see that it's suddenly two a.m.

Impermanence

One of the sometimes distressing facts about the Web is that no one guarantees to keep any information mounted indefinitely. An article or image that you thought was good enough to bookmark may not be there the next time you click on that link. You may get one of those unfriendly "Error 404: Not Found" messages, or you may find that the page is still there but has been updated, without the item you wanted. Most information on the Web is not as ephemeral as is

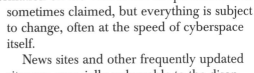

sometimes claimed, but everything is subject to change, often at the speed of cyberspace itself.

News sites and other frequently updated sites are especially vulnerable to the disappearance of information. Most online newspapers archive their articles, but other sites sometimes do not. The rapidly changing world brought on by information technology produces an exaggerated effect of outdatedness–the idea that 1996 was just after the age of covered wagons, so there is little use in keeping information created then.

Usage Tip

To guard yourself against the impermanence (and occasional ephemerality) of the Web, print out the valuable articles and images you locate. You will then have a permanent record, together with the URL, of your information, which you can then read, annotate, and quote from at leisure.

Gresham's Law of Information

If you have studied economics, you may have come across Gresham's Law: Bad money drives out good. Debased currency tends to take over, while the true specie disappears. An often raised concern among media watchers is that something similar may be happening to the information on the Web: Those sites with lower standards of truth, accuracy, or journalistic ethics are more willing than traditional media to spread half-truths, rumors, and gossip. Because of the perceived pressures of competition and the desire to be first with a hot story, traditional media outlets are finding it necessary to repeat many of these items. The burning issues here are two: (1) Must the Web necessarily have lower standards for truth than the traditional media? And (2) Is the Web reducing all news media to the lower standards of the tabloid press, which wallows in gossip, rumor, and innuendo?

A response to the first issue might be found in the example of a traditional bookstore. The books there have widely varying standards: some are very reliable, while others are little more than packaged gossip. The Web, like many traditional media outlets, also has a wide range in the quality of information available. (See chapter 5 on evaluation for help in assessing the quality of material on the Web.)

The answer to the second question is less clear, because competitive pressures have caused the traditional media to rush to publicize several questionable items from Web sources, and current debate suggests that this trend may continue. For the sake of truth and fairness, we can hope that all media outlets will eventually place being right over being first. (One rumor and gossip site on the Web claims that eighty percent of the items published there are true. Is that a fact worth bragging about? Would you read a daily newspaper that claimed, "Eighty percent of the stories we print are true—only twenty percent did not happen"?)

Web optimists note that the danger of declining standards applies mainly to news and news-related sites, which comprise only a rather small percentage of information on the Web.

Privacy and Safety

A well-known young film actress was recently sued as a result of a minor traffic accident. The filing of the suit and its supporting documents are, by law, public information. In the past, very few people would actually see this information, because obtaining it required a trip to the courthouse. Now, however, the information is only a few mouse clicks away because the documents have been posted to the Web. One of those posted documents is the original traffic ticket. Anyone with access to the Web can now learn not only the height, weight, eye color, and age of that actress, but her home address, driver's license number, automobile license plate number, and telephone number. In an age when stalkers seem all too common, the publication of this information seems to be a shocking and dangerous invasion of privacy.

The risk of invasion of privacy is much more personal than that, however. Whenever you use the Web, there is the possibility that information about you is being collected. Unlike the traditional information sources (newspapers, magazines, television), which allow you to consult them anonymously, many Web sites ask information about you and record your visits. You may be asked to register before you can use a site, or to provide some kind of personal information. Be very careful about what information you give out about yourself, especially if you are not familiar with the site owner.

To help keep yourself safe on the Web, follow these guidelines:

Do Not Give Personal Information to Strangers. Do not give your address, telephone number, any passwords, or credit card number(s) to someone you do not know about. Most especially, never give your Social Security number out over the Web. Often you will be asked to give your name and e-mail address as part of registration to use a site. In each case, you must decide if the risk of receiving junk e-mail is worth having access to the site. Usually, well-known commercial sites that require registration (such as the New York Times at *www.nytimes.com*) are safe enough. However, if you arrive at a small, unknown site, be a bit wary.

The same advice holds true for e-commerce–buying online. Well-known online businesses like Amazon.com (*www.amazon.com*) or CDNow (*www.cdnow.com*) have developed track records of trustworthiness and customer satisfaction, so you can feel safe giving your credit card number and shipping address to them. Once again, though, be careful about unfamiliar sites.

A final area where you might inadvertently give information to strangers is through a mailing list. Listservs allow users to post information bulletin-board style, where an e-mail you write will be forwarded to hundreds or even thousands of other people. Remember,

Usage Tip

Some sites allow you the option to let them "remember" your password and user ID to get access to their site. The information is stored in what is called a "cookie" on the computer you are using at the time. If you use various school computers, you should refuse to have your password remembered, both because it will be remembered only on the computer you are currently using, and because anyone else using that computer in the future can use your login information to access that site.

then, that if you post a message (through e-mail, a Web feedback form, or other means), it may be read by many other people.

Beware of Online Relationships. Yes, it is true that a number of people have met and gotten married through the Internet. It is also true that a number of people have met and gotten murdered through the Internet. There are predators and con artists in the "three dimensional" world as well, but the Internet, whether Web sites or chat rooms or even e-mail, allows disguise much more readily. There is a famous *New Yorker* cartoon that shows two dogs in front of a computer. One says to the other, "On the Internet, no one knows you're a dog." And there is a saying, "Half the 24-year-old women on the Internet are really 13-year-old boys." The claim is certainly an exaggeration, but the point is, you do not really know to whom you are talking when all you have is a chat room, Web site, or e-mail message. Be a bit skeptical and use good judgment about developing such relationships.

Citing Sources

The purpose of this book is to help you find high quality, reliable information for use in research papers, reports, and presentations. As you are surely aware, whenever you use information from any source, Web or otherwise, you must cite that source. You should be happy to do this, because citing your sources provides several benefits, both to you and to your reader.

Cite to Acknowledge Credit. Citing acknowledges and honors the rightful creator of the intellectual property you are using. More than that, however, citation shows that you are engaged in the world of ideas, in the interchange of ideas. It shows that you are aware of other people's discussion of the issue you are treating, and that you are not writing in an intellectual vacuum. The fact is, then, that citation actually strengthens your writing, by showing that your arguments have the support of other thoughtful people, that you are aware of countervailing arguments, and that you are engaged in some aspect of "the great conversation" about an issue of interest to others as well.

Cite to Avoid Plagiarism. Citation of your sources protects you from charges of plagiarism or even copyright infringement. Nothing weakens an argument more than intellectual dishonesty, and few professors are willing to accept an explanation of accidental copying or ignorance of the nature of plagiarism. As a handy reminder, then, the rules for avoiding plagiarism are as follows:

✶ You must put quotation marks around all the words you take from another source, and cite the source clearly.

✶ When you paraphrase or summarize a source, you must use your own words completely, show clearly where the paraphrase begins and ends, and cite the source clearly.

✶ Always clearly distinguish between your own ideas and comments and the ideas of others you are using.

Cite to Help Your Reader. Another purpose of citation is to provide information for the benefit of your reader. Of necessity, your quotations must remain brief, while something you quote may spur your reader's interest to find out more about the subject in the original material . Your citation enables the reader to locate the source of the quotation or paraphrase and to read the full account from which you selected just a sentence or so. Your reader can verify the information, see its context, or most importantly, do further reading about that idea.

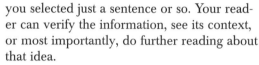

Citation Styles

There are several styles for citing references from the Web. Covered in this chapter are MLA (Modern Language Association), APA (American Psychological Association), and CM (Chicago Manual of Style). All three of these citation styles have the same goal—crediting sources in a way that makes it easy for a reader to locate them. For Web references, the most critical part of the citation is the URL (Uniform Resource Locator, the Web address). Be especially careful, then, to copy it exactly. Good advice is to use cut and paste to avoid transcription errors and then to test the URL by typing it into your browser just as you have recorded it in your bibliography.

Those who post information to the Web do not always appear to be thinking about how the information can be cited. As a result, you may find that some parts of a standard citation

Usage Tip

For many citations, the article itself will not provide all the information you need. You will have to go back to a title page or to the Web site's home page to gather some information. Record this information when you first determine that the article will be of use to you. Otherwise, you may have to go back online and look up what you need.

are missing. This problem is not new to citation practice, however. Many books (especially some older ones) lack a publication date or publisher name or author name. Your goal, then, is to gather as many parts as you can (and most especially an accurate URL), and then not to worry about parts you cannot find. In the examples below, some of the most common situations will be discussed, to show you how to locate information and how to cite various pages.

You might want to read through the examples given for all three citation styles, because the citations are presented in narrative form as problem-solving exercises, which will give you some ideas about the strategies used for citing different kinds of Web information.

A Note on the Citation Styles in This Chapter. Online citation style is a new art and is still in the process of being refined. The styles described in this chapter are the most current ones available at press time. If you compare the specifics with those in books published as recently as 1997, you will notice some differences, because both the MLA and APA have refined their Web citation formats recently, and that of the Chicago Manual is still under development.

Citing Sources MLA Style

For its citation style, the Modern Language Association uses an in-text reference which directs the reader to a list of Works Cited at the end of the article. For printed works, the in-text reference includes the author's last name and page number. For Web citations, where few Web documents have page numbers, you can give either a section or paragraph number (if those exist in the document) or simply the author's last name. Here is an example:

A spa chemistry expert recommends adding spa shock after using the spa "in order to help assure a sanitizer level in the water" (Schuster).

Then, in your Works Cited, you include as much of the information from the list below as is needed. In this example, Mr. Schuster maintains a sub-site called Ask Alan on the Aqua-Clear Industries Web site. His article, "Spa and Hot Tub Chemical Questions," was last updated on August 18, 1998. It was accessed (and in fact, the article was printed off) on October 10, 1998. Putting all of this information together, along with the exact URL of the article (not of the home page), the reference will look like this:

Schuster, Alan. "Spa and Hot Tub Chemical Questions." *Ask Alan.*
    18 Aug. 1998. Aqua-Clear Industries. 10 Oct. 1998
    <http://www.aqua-clear.com/alan/aa9.htm>.

The MLA format for what to include in a Works Cited entry is as follows. Use, in this order, as many of these items as are relevant, useful—and available—for clearly identifying the source document. The list is long not so that you will include all of it in every reference, but because Web page content and format vary so widely.

1. Last name, then first name of the author or editor of the article.
2. Title of the article in quotation marks.
3. Site name or site section that has collected the articles, or book title, either underlined or italicized.
4. Editor or compiler's name (if not used in No. 1 above).
5. Publication information for the printed version, if such exists.
6. Title of Web site (if No. 3 is a site section), project, or database. Use Home Page if no title.
7. Editor of the Web site or project or database, if any.
8. Version number, volume number, or other identifying number.
9. Date of publication, posting, or modification.
10. Total pages, sections, or paragraphs if numbered.
11. Name of corporation, organization, or institution sponsoring Web site.
12. Date when you accessed the site.
13. URL of the document <in angle brackets> followed by a period.

Usage Tip

You will often find sites where the site name and organization are the same, so that you can omit the organization name. The result is that the article date and your date of access are right next to each other. It may look strange, but it is MLA style.

Note from the example above that you will normally be using only about half a dozen of these. The usual format will be like this:

Lastname, Firstname. "Article Title." *Site Name.* Article date. Organization Name. Date of access <URL>.

Here are some examples of the more common references you will encounter.

Example 1: You find an article on e-mail tracking hoaxes on an urban legends site connected to the Mining Company. The maintainer of the site is the author. There is even a date of posting for the article. It is cited in this way:

Emery, David. "Further Adventures in Email Tracking." *Your Mining Co. Guide to Urban Legends and Folklore.* 12 Aug 1998. The Mining Company. 14 Oct. 1998 <http://urbanlegends.miningco.com/library/weekly/aa081298.htm>.

Example 2: Looking for information on feeding babies, you arrive at the Gerber Baby Food Web site and read an article on "Newborn Feeding." There is no author and no date. (Even the "View," "Page Info" procedure in Netscape yields no date information.) It is cited in-text in this way:

In an article, "Newborn Feeding," the Gerber Baby Food company notes that for the first three to five days of breast feeding, a woman's body "will produce a substance called colostrum. This thick, yellowy substance is a milk rich in antibodies. . . ."

In the Works Cited it is listed this way:

"Newborn Feeding." *Welcome to Gerber.* Gerber Corporation. 18 Oct. 1998 <http://www.gerber.com/phases/newborn/feeding.html>.

Example 3: While searching for information on fox hunting, you arrive at chapter three of the online book, *The Legacy of the Horse.* There is no author, but there are section titles. You use it this way:

According to the "Fox Hunt" section of chapter three of *The Legacy of the Horse,* wire fencing is "the anathema to fox hunters."

There is no date on the work, but looking at "View," "Page Info" reveals a "Last Modified" date of November 21, 1997. Your citation looks like this:

"Chapter 3: 1680-1840: Racing in England—The Demise of the English Stage Coach." *The Legacy of the Horse.* 21 Nov. 1997. International Museum of the Horse. 18 Oct. 1998 <http://www.imh.org/imh/kyhpl3b.html>.

Example 4: During research about urban planning, you locate "The Ahwahnee Principles." No author is stated, but the principles are numbered. You use the source in this way:

According to the "Ahwahnee Principles" for good urban design, "The community design should help conserve resources and minimize waste" (Principle 13).

By clicking on the "Return to the Center's home page" choice on the article page, you learn that the Principles come from The Center for Livable Communities, which you also learn is a sub-site and daughter organization of the Local Government Commission, owner of the Web site *www.lgc.org*. A "View," "Page Info" check on the Netscape browser also reveals a "Last Modified" date of August 18, 1997 for the Principles page. Note that Internet Explorer returns only the date the article was translated to your disc or hard drive when you click on "File," "Properties." Your citation will therefore look like this:

"The Ahwahnee Principles." *The Center for Livable Communities.* 18 Aug. 1997. 23 Principles. Local Government Commission. 18 Oct. 1998 <http://www.lgc.org/clc/ahwan.html>.

For some additional examples and advice, see the Modern Language Association's "MLA Style" article at *www.mla.org/main_stl-nf.htm*.

Citing Sources APA Style

APA in-text citation style uses a parenthetical reference to the author's last name and the date of the article. If there are page numbers and if the reference is to a particular page (rather than to the entire article), then the page number should be included also.

The bibliography page in APA style is called "References." The reference style should include the following for Web sources:

1. Author's last name, then first initial (or organization name, if corporate author).
2. Date of publication (year, or year first, followed by month or month and day).
3. Article title or book title.
4. Journal title, if any.
5. Description of information type, in brackets. For example, [On-line newspaper].

6. Web site or sub-site.
7. The phrase, "Retrieved *date* from the World Wide Web:"
8. URL with no period at the end.

Note then that the usual citation format will look like this:

Lastname, First Initial. (Publication Date). Article Title. [On-line type]. *Web site.* Retrieved month-day-year from the World Wide Web: URL

Example 1: Jorge Villegas has mounted a Web site on emotion and advertising. You arrive at his article, "Advertising Processing," and want to cite it. There is no name or visible date. A "View," "Page Info" check with the Netscape browser reveals the "Last Modified" date as October 11, 1997. Clicking on the "Home" selection at the bottom of the article takes you to the home page, "Welcome to the Emotion and Advertising Web Site," where you see the author's name. Putting this information together, you have the APA reference as follows. Note the special style of presentation:

Villegas, J. (1997, October 11). Advertising processing. [On-line article]. *Welcome to the Emotion and Advertising Web Site.* Retrieved October 19, 1998 from the World Wide Web: http://uts.cc.utexas.edu/ ~ad382jv/ea/adver.html

The above example reveals that the article title is not surrounded by quotation marks, and that only the first word is capitalized. The word "on-line" is hyphenated in APA style. There is no period after the URL.

Example 2: You locate the online book, *Schizophrenia: A Handbook for Families.* The author in this case is an organization, Health Canada, and the site has been mounted by Internet Mental Health. You will list it in this way:

Health Canada. (1997, September 17). *Schizophrenia: A handbook for families.* [On-line book]. Internet Mental Health. Retrieved October 19, 1998 from the World Wide Web: http://www.mentalhealth.com/ book/p40-sc01.html

Example 3: You search the archives of the *Kansas City Star* online for articles about the antidepressant Prozac and come across a story about psychologists in Missouri who want the legal right to write prescriptions. You use it in your paper this way:

Psychologists in Missouri are "pressing for the right to prescribe psychoactive drugs, those used to treat depression, anxiety and other mental disorders" (Uhlenhuth, 1998, October 4).

The References page records the citation this way:

Uhlenhuth, K. (1998, October 4). Psychologists penning prescriptions? Experts disagree on whether to give power to therapists without medical degrees. *Kansas City Star.* [Newspaper, article in archives]. Retrieved October 20, 1998 from the World Wide Web: http://www.kcstar.com/sbin/iarecord?NS-doc-path=/vol1/pubs/archive-98/9810/981004/981004.068&NS-collection=archive-98&NS-search-set=/var/tmp/362be/aaaa005SJ2bef3d&NS-doc-offset=1&

Example 4: For the final APA example, let us use the article from the Gerber Web site cited above under MLA style, to see the difference in bibliographic entry. Since the page has no listed date, the date of access is given in parentheses. The APA entry would look like this:

Newborn feeding. (1998, October 20). [On-line article]. *Welcome to Gerber.* Retrieved October 20, 1998 from the World Wide Web: http://www.gerber.com/phases/newborn/feeding.html

For some additional examples, see "How to Cite Information From the Internet and the World Wide Web," on the APA Web site at *www.apa.org/journals/webref.html.*

Citing Sources Chicago Manual Style

The Chicago Manual of Style documentation system includes both a full bibliography footnote entry at the bottom of the page where information is cited and a bibliographic reference page at the end. For convenience, the examples here include both types of entry. For Chicago, the information to be included should be in this order:

Usage Tip

The URL in the example above is so long that it is abbreviated on a hardcopy printout of the article, and does not entirely show in the address window of the browser. To capture the address accurately, click in the address window to highlight the URL and then choose "Edit," "Copy." Now go to your word processor and paste the URL into the appropriate place or into a temporary file for use later.

1. Author's name.
2. Title of article in quotation marks.
3. Web site, journal or book title, italicized.
4. Date of document.
5. Type of online source, in brackets. For example, [abstract online].
6. The URL, preceded by "Available from."
7. Date of access, preceded by "accessed."

Note, then, that a typical note and citation will look like this:

1. Firstname Lastname, "Article Title," *Web site,* day-month-year [online type]; available from URL; accessed day-month-year.

Lastname, Firstname. "Article Title." *Web site,* day-month-year. Online type. Available from URL; accessed day-month-year.

Note in the examples (above and below) the differing punctuation used for the footnote and the bibliography:

Example 1: You locate an article about Rembrandt on the WebMuseum, Paris site. You use it this way:

According to Nicolas Pioch, Rembrandt produced "approximately 600 paintings, 300 etchings, and 1,400 drawings."[1]

The entries look like this:

1. Nicolas Pioch, "Rembrandt," *WebMuseum, Paris,* 16 Feb 1996 [article online]; available from http://sunsite.unc.edu/wm/paint/auth/rembrandt/; accessed 22 Jan 1999.

Pioch, Nicolas. "Rembrandt." *WebMuseum, Paris,* 16 Feb 1996. Article online. Available from http://sunsite.unc.edu/wm/paint/auth/rembrandt/; accessed 22 Jan 1999.

Example 2: Your search takes you to an article on Russian social movements. An author is listed but no date. Using "View," "Page Info," you get a document date of February 7, 1996. By backing up, you discover that the article belongs to a monograph which has been mounted by the Centre for Social Anthropology and Computing and that the monograph has a 1991 date on it. The note and citation look like this:

2. Sergey Mamay, "Theories of Social Movements and Their Current Development in Soviet Society," in Jerry Eades and Caroline Schwaller, eds., *Transitional Agendas: Working Papers from the Summer School for Soviet Sociologists*, 1991. *Centre for Social Anthropology and Computing*, University of Kent at Canterbury, 7 Feb 1996 [monograph online]; available from http://lucy.ukc.ac.uk/csacpub/csacmonog.html; accessed 16 Dec 1998.

Mamay, Sergey. "Theories of Social Movements and Their Current Development in Soviet Society." In Jerry Eades and Caroline Schwaller, eds., *Transitional Agendas: Working Papers from the Summer School for Soviet Sociologists*, 1991. *Centre for Social Anthropology and Computing*, University of Kent at Canterbury, 7 Feb 1996. Monograph online. Available from http://lucy.ukc.ac.uk/csacpub/csacmonog.html; accessed 16 Dec 1998.

Example 3: While researching the Dark Ages, you find an abstract of an article from *Archaeology* magazine, complete with author, date, and even a preferred URL. Here are the note and citation:

3. Richard Hodges, "The Not-So-Dark Ages," *Archaeology*, September/October 1998 [abstract online]; available from http://www.archaeolgy.org/9809/abstracts/darkages.html; accessed 4 Feb 1999.

Hodges, Richard. "The Not-So-Dark Ages." *Archaeology*, September/October 1998. Abstract online. Available from http://www/archaeolgy.org/9809/abstracts/darkages.html; accessed 4 Feb 1999.

Example 4: While researching for information about how to raise capital for a small business, you locate an article published by the Securities and Exchange Commission. The article date says "April 1997," but at the end is a note that it was last updated on December 19, 1997. In this case, the corporate author and the name of the Web site are the same. Using the most recent date, your note and citation will look like this:

4. U. S. Securities and Exchange Commission, "Q&A: Small Business and the SEC," *U. S. Securities and Exchange Commission*, 19 Dec 1997 [online article]; available from http://www.sec.gov/smbus/qasbsec.htm; accessed 14 Jan 1999.

U.S. Securities and Exchange Commission. "Q&A: Small Business and the SEC." *U. S. Securities and Exchange Commission,* 19 Dec 1997. Online article. Available from http://www.sec.gov/smbus/qasbsec.htm; accessed 14 Jan 1999.

Citing Special Cases

Citing Non-Text Items. For all of the citation styles above, cite images, sounds, video clips, banner ads, and even icons by the page on which they are found. Just as a photograph in a book would be cited by referring to the photograph and then citing the book, the same strategy is useful for the non-text portions of Web pages. For example, here is an MLA-style citation of a photograph:

This example of a red-eyed tree frog clearly shows the balled toes (Loosemore).

Since there is no date available for the page, the Works Cited entry would look like this:

Loosemore, Sandra. "More Froggy Images (page 1)." The Froggy Page. 14 Feb 1999 <http://frog.simplenet.com/froggy/images-1.shtml>.

Remember that an important reason for citing sources is to allow the reader to locate not just the idea (or image) but the context. Citing just the exact URL of the image, then, would not help the reader see the context of its presentation.

Citing a Page with Multiple URLs. The same page of information may be available with more than one URL for one of two reasons. First, there may be mirror sites for the information. Mirror sites contain copies of the same Web pages so that heavily accessed information will not overload a single server. Often mirror sites are located in widely separated geographical areas. The DataFellows

Usage Tip

While images are often identified on the Web page itself, sometimes they are not. HTML permits an optional <alt> tag to provide a title for an image, in the event that the image either does not load or the user has images turned off in the browser. If the tag is present, it will display before the image loads, or you can turn off images and then reload the page. (You can also choose "View," "Document Source" and read the tag in the HTML document.) Sometimes all you will find is the name of the image file, but often you will find a useful name.

antivirus site, for example, has mirror sites in both the United States and in Europe. The second reason the same information may have more than one URL is that some sites allow the same actual Web site to be accessed through more than one address. For example, you can access Disneyland's home page by using either *www.disneyland.com* or *www.disney.com/Disneyland*. The latter is the actual URL, while the former is a forwarding URL. Whenever possible, cite the actual URL.

Occasionally, you find a URL mentioned at the bottom of a Web page. In such cases, you should test the URL first, and if it brings you to the same page, use it in your bibliography. The address you used to access the page first may be a "click-through" or forwarding address rather than the actual address, or the address in the "Location" window may be that of the frameset instead of the page itself (see the next entry).

Citing a Page in a Frameset. Frames allow Web site creators to display multiple small windows on your browser screen, where each window can display information independent of the others. Sometimes one window will have a menu in it with choices that display items in another window. This collection of interoperable frames is called a frameset. The unfortunate problem for researchers is that the frameset URL stays in the browser "Location" area regardless of the sub-windows chosen. Sometimes site creators put the URL for the article at the bottom of the article with a note, such as, "The URL for this page is www.snopes.com/spoons/legends/pulltab.htm. Please use this URL in all links or references to this page." Occasionally, the site creator will put the URL in the message area at the bottom of the browser screen (the area that normally says "Document Done"). A third way to discover the actual URL of an article in a frame window is to print it out. Both Netscape and Internet Explorer print the actual page URL on each page of the article. Lastly, you can click on "View," "Page Info," and look at the contents of the frameset, where all the URLs should be listed.

If you have tried all of these methods and still cannot find the address you want, you will have no choice but to use the frameset URL.

For example, suppose you visit the *Virtual Autopsy* site and look at "Case 3." There you find a photograph of a blood film. As you have clicked through the autopsy information, the URL has remained the same, at *www.le.ac.uk/pathology/teach/VA/case_3/frmst3.html*. You could use this address for your bibliography, but by printing out the page,

"Reticulo-Endothelial System," which contains the photograph, you note that the page URL is *www.le.ac.uk/pathology/teach/VA/case_3/ meming7.html*. Since you now have an exact address for the page, that is the one you should use.

——>◆<——

Copyright Issues

There are two possibly surprising facts about copyright law that may affect how you use the Web in your work.

It's All Copyrighted

The first fact is that *everything that is written down is automatically copyrighted*. The writing does not need to be registered anywhere, nor does it have to contain a copyright notice. The implication of this fact is that every Web page you see, every newsgroup posting you read in a Web archive, every e-mail you receive from a Web author (or anyone else) is a copyrighted work. True, there are some works now in the public domain and no longer copyrighted, but these are almost all very old works (such as eighteenth century novels). Everything new—unless it is just a phrase or is explicitly declared to be in the public domain—is copyrighted.

The restriction this puts on you is that you cannot publish someone else's copyrighted work. Suppose, for example, that you are assigned a research paper that you must post to a Web site as part of the assignment. Suppose also that you have received an e-mail from a Web site creator commenting on something you asked about in an article you are quoting. Under copyright law, you cannot post the e-mail to your own Web site without the permission of the author. (And you should not quote it in your research paper unless you get permission.) You may not repost any writings, images, tables, graphs, or sounds created by others without their explicit permission.

You Have Fair Use

Copyright law makes clear provision for the fair use of copyrighted works for educational purposes. For your academic research projects, you have the right to print copies of Web pages, quote from them, and reproduce images, tables, and graphs for assignments you are submitting to a professor. However, as mentioned earlier, you may not repost this information to the Web. If your assignment includes creating a Web page for the report, be careful what you put on it and secure permission to mount any images, articles, or other entire "works." If you simply turn in a traditional paper, then reproducing a summary page, a sidebar (a short article connected to a longer article), or other item that might constitute copyright infringement if you published it, is permitted under the fair use principle. Just remember that each reproduction needs to be cited.

For more information on copyright law, see the US Copyright Office at *lcweb.loc.gov/copyright/* and Cyberspace Law for Non-Lawyers at *www.ssm.com/update/lsn/cyberspace/csl_lessons.html.*

Chapter 7

Thinking Critically in a World of Information

⟶⟫●⟪⟵

Words are, of course, the most powerful drug used by mankind.
                                                    –Rudyard Kipling

Man is obviously made in order to think; it is the whole of his digni-
ty and merit, and his whole duty is to think as he ought. –Blaise Pascal

⟶⟫●⟪⟵

Why Is Critical Thinking Necessary?

Critical thinking is both an attitude and a process–an attitude that
favors the exploration and assessment of ideas, and a process of
active and deliberate consideration of ideas, as opposed to a passive
acceptance of them. You hold an idea at arm's length and examine it
before accepting it into your mental framework. You say to a conclusion, "Okay, now show me the evidence." Another way of defining
critical thinking might be as a habit of cautious evaluation, an analytic
mindset aimed at discovering the component parts of ideas and
philosophies, and weighing the merits of arguments and reasons in
order to become a good judge of them. Analysis is the ability to break
arguments or claims down into parts and to discover the relationship
between them. The arguments can then more readily be evaluated.
 Especially as a user of the Web, you should develop the habit of
thinking critically because the Web is home to such a wide range of
information, available for many different purposes.

Information as a Commodity

Information has always been created to inform, educate, or
persuade others, and much of the information on the Web exists

for these reasons. Then, too, information has always been something of a commodity, to be packaged and sold (in books or magazines, for example). More recently, however, the value of information as truth or as an accurate representation of reality is increasingly being subordinated to its value as a commercial product. Thus, information is shaped, processed, and packaged to meet the needs and desires of the consumer. For this reason, information users and evaluators need to consider the source, audience, and purpose of information when determining its value. Information on the Web is subject to the same pressures from advertising and entertainment values as information in other media. And just as junk food is often as popular as nutritious food, we should not be surprised that junk information is popular along with quality information.

You are probably already aware of the way truth and fiction, or information and advertising are blended in some of the programming on television. Infomercials are advertisements dressed like talk shows or news magazines; docudramas are quasi-historical teleplays that fictionalize historical events; infotainment blends information and entertainment; edutainment similarly mixes teaching goals with amusement. Information on the Web has similar variety. Some links on a page may be there as genuine information sources, while others exist because the Web site was paid to include them. Recognizing this diversity of purposes is a first step toward assessing the credibility of each source.

Information as a Tool or Weapon

All of us use information to make decisions, often involving money, voting, believing, supporting, or opposing an idea. It follows, then, that information that helps shape our decisions has considerable power. Just as accurate information can help us make good decisions, wrong or distorted information can be used to manipulate us into making decisions we would not otherwise make. Some information sources have as their goal not to provide objective data but to change our attitudes or behavior. For example, spin doctors are a professional class of information workers who deliberately try to convince us of a particular point of view. But spin doctors, unscrupulous salesmen, dishonest politicians, and counterspies are not the only ones who use information to fool us. Advertisers, corporations, organizations, even our friends, may at times have some interest in shaping our beliefs or decision making, and they may attempt to do this by manipulating the information we receive from them. A lie is the most blatant example of this.

But partial truth can be an even more effective weapon. Information can be selected, slanted, distorted, falsified, or reinterpreted. It is not uncommon, especially among less-sophisticated commercial Web sites, for the producer of some item (natural cosmetics or food supplements, for example) to claim not only that the company's products are wonderful in every way but that its competitors' products are somehow inferior or even harmful. A critical consideration, then, is not only to assess the idea but also the reliability and authority of the source. For example, in the statement "Green tea is good for you," it is important to assess *who says* "Green tea is good for you." Is that source believable or is it perhaps speaking from financial self-interest?

Critical Thinking Tip

Along with considering the "what" of information (what the information is about) think about the "who" and the "why." Who created this and why?

Biases Affecting Information

One of the well-established principles of marketing is that most consumers do not distinguish between the product and the package. To them the package represents the product. The same thing is true when the product is information; we seldom receive it in an objective or neutral way. Instead, there are several biases that affect the degree of influence a given amount of information has on our knowledge, beliefs, and decision making. Here, briefly, are some of those biases as they relate to Web information.

Availability

We are more likely to be influenced by information that is already present, handy, or easy to find than by information that requires effort to locate it. The battle account in the encyclopedia at your elbow is more likely to be read (and influence your beliefs) than the account in the encyclopedia in the next room. The availability bias is a serious problem in Web research, since there is always the temptation to take the first few hits resulting from a search and look no further. The problem is that the hits down the list or the information that takes more effort to locate may actually be the more reliable or the more definitive in making good decisions. After all, some sites manipulate their Web pages to assure a higher ranking in search engine lists than the search would otherwise produce because higher ranking means more hits, and more hits mean more potential profits, either from direct sales at the site or from advertising dollars, which are based on hits. If someone is willing to produce an artificial ranking on a search engine, what else might be going on with the information on the page?

It is easy to be lazy and just take what is handy. Many of us are already finding that we will take what we can find on the Internet rather than supplement this information with what we can find in printed resources.

Packaging

Bankers learned long ago that customers wanted to feel that their bank was solid and secure, so banks were built out of stone and granite (or at least a veneer!) to look serious, weighty, and safe. Many Web sites use this packaging concept to look solid, serious, and credible. The design, graphics, and overall presentation create an aura of professionalism and reliability. However, with the easy-to-use Web page creation software now available, almost anyone can create pages with the appearance of substance and truth. And, on the other side, a site with a rather humble appearance may contain highly valuable information. A gardener who has spent twenty years raising bromeliads may mount a site with only modest appearance while a mail order firm with little experience may have a very slick site. As the cyberspace proverb tells us, "Beauty is only screen deep."

Visual Presentation

Information presented visually often influences us more than information presented textually. Visual items are immediate, graphic, colorful, and do not require the processing that reading does. Hence, the Chinese proverb, "A picture is worth a thousand words." And because the Web supports multimedia and pictures are an integral part of the experience, we have a tendency to assume that pictures support the claims made by the text, but that is not always the case. Be careful not to be overly swayed by the graphics, but make sure you base your judgment on the text or data underlying the graphics. It is also a good idea to ask yourself whether or not the graphics fairly represent the information.

Recency

We all have so much information flowing into our consciousness every day that we just cannot keep track of all of it. New information pushes out old. We therefore tend to favor the most recently gained information, and base our decisions (and change our minds) because of this "new" information. Had the information arrived in a different order, our decision might have been different. This bias is especially prominent in the realm of Web research, where it is possible to locate vast quantities of information about a given topic. The treatment for this bias is to look at your printouts or notes regularly, so that newer information will not automatically enjoy a privileged position of influence.

Confirmation

The confirmation bias arises after some research has been completed or after a hypothesis has been formed. Instead of searching for more information of any kind on an issue, the researcher begins to look only for information that supports (or confirms) the emerging hypothesis. As a consequence, information that conflicts with the hypothesis is depreciated or even misinterpreted. Advice given to business executives suggests that once an idea begins to form, they should seek disconfirming information as well as confirming information. That advice would serve well for Web research also.

Dramatic Narrative

Many people base their personal behavior and values on generalizations formed by single personal experiences, even when those generalizations conflict with much better established facts based on thorough empirical investigation. Abstract truths, detailed statistics, even moral values—all are ignored when a strong personal experience points to a different conclusion. The emotion attached to the experience, the reality of it all, and the feeling of being an eyewitness, are too much to confute. It is no wonder so many people who have something to sell seem bent on giving us the "razzle dazzle" instead of cogent arguments or facts. But if you have watched any magic acts or demonstrations of "miracle" products, you know that substance and style are not necessarily the same. Be careful, then, of Web pages that rely excessively on anecdotes or testimonials rather than on facts and arguments.

Privilege

Information we are convinced is scarce, secret, special, or restricted takes on an automatically greater value and appears more credible than information that just anybody can obtain. Similarly, information that requires effort or expense is viewed as being more valuable or reliable. You can imagine that the manipulators have long ago caught on to this particular bias, and use it to make us want or believe something that otherwise would make us yawn. Be very skeptical of sites that claim exclusive information or information that is restricted. Just remember, a book commonly found in Las Vegas casino shops is titled, *The Book the Casinos Don't Want You to Read.*

Using Rival Hypotheses

A hypothesis is a proposed explanation for a collection of data. By nature a hypothesis goes beyond the evidence at hand and seeks to combine the facts into some relationship of cause and effect, source and influence, intention or meaning. Since hypotheses are always only probable, there is always some danger that a given hypothesis or explanation may not be the correct one. A rival hypothesis is an alternative explanation for the same set of facts or data, another way of explaining the same results or events. When you begin to examine a proposed explanation for some data, ask yourself, "What other factors are involved that might also account for the result?"

You can construct rival hypotheses for the data you find on the Web to help you determine the strength or probability of a conclusion given to you. You can develop as many rival hypotheses as possible for each set of data, and then test each of the hypotheses against the known facts. Keep in mind that the supporters of a given hypothesis may reveal only the facts that support it. You may have to do some research and visit other sites to find additional evidence that may point in other directions.

Here are some guidelines for hypothesis testing:

★ The hypothesis should account for all possibly relevant data. There will often be small anomalies that do not seem to fit the strongest hypothesis, but the hypothesis should be consistent with all the important facts.

★ Simpler and more probable explanations are usually to be preferred over more complex and less probable ones (this is the rule of Occam's Razor, also called the law of parsimony). The moving glow in the sky may come from a UFO, but an airplane landing light should be considered first.

★ If the hypothesis is true, the consequences following from it must match the facts. (A fire implies the consequences of soot, for instance.)

As an example, suppose you read about a study concluding that coffee is linked to heart attacks. "People who drink more than six cups of coffee a day have more heart attacks than those who drink less," the study says. "This shows that drinking coffee causes heart attacks." Are there any rival hypotheses that might explain this correlation of events? What about these:

★ People who drink more than six cups of coffee a day may have a job that puts them under a lot of stress or requires them to keep alert, and the stress or need for alertness may be the causal factor in heart attacks.

★ Many people who drink coffee also light up a cigarette at the same time, so heavy coffee drinkers may be heavy smokers, and the heavier smoking may cause the increase in heart attacks.

★ Drinking more than six cups of coffee a day may cause pronounced insomnia and hence fatigue, resulting in poorer health and increased heart attacks.

★ If these heavy coffee drinkers also eat a donut or pastry with their coffee, they may have higher cholesterol or an overweight condition, either of which is a risk factor for heart attacks.

When more information becomes available, some hypotheses can be eliminated and more can be formed until one becomes the best (or even the only) explanation to fit all of the data. The point is, do not assume that a given conclusion is the only explanation for a set of data. Let the evidence convince you before you accept it.

Identifying Logical Fallacies

A logical fallacy is an error in an argument that makes the argument unacceptable because of how it is expressed, the contents of the expression, or some other flaw. Many times an argument will be expressed unfairly or shift the grounds of evidence.

Whether or not a particular argument commits a logical fallacy is often a matter for careful and discriminating judgment, because the fallacies can imitate right reasoning, or are excesses or abuses of legitimate argumentation.

Judging Between Legitimate and Fallacious Arguments

This section discusses several tensions between legitimate argument and fallacy relevant to Web information. These discussions should provide you with the thinking tools useful for judging the information you will encounter.

Legitimate Use of Authority Versus the Fallacy of the Appeal to Prestige. Because we cannot personally check out every claim to fact, we must take the word of others for much of what we know. For us to accept another's word, we expect that person to be an authority in the field. In other words, most of our knowledge is based on an appeal to authority. However, such an appeal can become fallacious when the authority fails to support a claim reasonably with arguments and evidence. The fallacy of the Appeal to Prestige lies in associating an argument or conclusion merely with the fame or reputation of some person or organization, thus making a relationship between status and proof. The argument is intended to take advantage of an audience's ignorance by exploiting its respect for authority.

An appeal to authority can be reasonably grounded when the authority bases his or her conclusions on observations, experiments, knowledge, educated judgment, or some set of reasons. The judgments of experts are essential components of our knowledge. The problem is that it is not always easy to tell when an appeal to authority is reasonably grounded and when the fame of the asserter is being substituted for arguments or evidence.

We find some of the most frequent occurrences of the fallacious Appeal to Prestige in areas of controversy, where certain complex truths remain only partially understood. Whenever a prestigious organization issues a new study or even an opinion, those who agree with the report's conclusions praise it as the final truth and demand credence for it because its authors are prestigious. Thus what should have been an ongoing factual debate is rendered a mere battle of reputations. "You should believe my truth because I have more famous people supporting it than my opponents have famous people supporting their truth." Many legal cases involve battles like this between competing camps of experts.

Here are some ideas to keep in mind when considering or evaluating an appeal to authority:

1. *Equally respectable authorities often give conflicting opinions.* If one group of competent people is opposed to another, whether the opposition is large or small, a mere authority

appeal will not be sufficient for supporting a point.

2. *Some realms of knowledge are better for the use of authorities or experts than others.* The opinion of an authority on auto repair, chemistry, or electric power generation (areas of reasonably exact knowledge) is much more likely to be useful and persuasive than the opinion of an authority on politics, social movements, or the psychology of television (areas of inexact knowledge). In these latter categories, the appeal too often amounts to a mere appeal to prestige.

3. *The authority may be wrong.* This is true even in areas of exact knowledge. We might think that scientists, for example, would always be careful to investigate and consider an issue before making a pronouncement. And yet scientists are human. William Harvey's discovery of the circulation of the blood met with prejudiced opposition from various authorities, as did Joseph Lister's argument for the use of antiseptics in surgery. The voice of authority supported belief in phlogiston (an old theory that regarded fire as possessing material substance). For many years, dozens of observers "saw" canals full of water on Mars, and the theory of continental drift was once ridiculed by many geologists.

Critical Thinking Tip

Test the experts by looking at how carefully they use data to support their positions and how reasonably they present their cases. One especially good test is to see how fair an expert is to conclusions that conflict with the expert's own.

As you search the Web, then, do indeed look for authoritative sites and information. But do not let authoritative sites and comments keep you from doing your own thinking and analysis. Test the evidence and arguments presented against your own knowledge and against the other information you are finding.

Collaborative Filtering Versus the Fallacy of *Argumentum ad Populum.* With the explosion of worldwide information, whether it is the hundreds of millions of pages mounted on the Web or the tens of thousands of books published each year, all of us are looking for techniques that simplify the assessment of information. One of those techniques to emerge has been collaborative filtering. Essentially, collaborative filtering relies on the combined analysis and decisions

Critical Thinking Tip

Use collaborative filtering as a guide, not as a final authority.

of others to provide judgments or rankings about information. Because computer power makes it easy, collaborative filtering has become quite popular on the Web. For example, the online bookstore, Amazon.com (*www.Amazon.com*) allows prospective book buyers to read book reviews posted by anyone. The store also shows the sales popularity of each book by a ranking. Similarly, the site 100Hot.com (*www.100Hot.com*) lists the one hundred most popular sites in various areas, such as sports, newspapers, jobs and so on. The one hundred most popular newspapers in the list include many excellent publications, making this a good example of the potential value of collaborative filtering.

Collaborative filtering allows us to answer the question, "What do others think, or what have others done, who got here before I did?" As such it can provide some helpful guidance through the morass of information.

However, there is a danger in drawing conclusions merely from popularity, and the *Argumentum ad Populum* fallacy (also known as the Appeal to the Masses or the Bandwagon Appeal), was long ago identified as a major method of leading people astray. This fallacy makes an appeal to a person's sense of wanting to belong, wanting to follow what others are doing in order to fit in and feel normal. Peer group pressure, fads, styles, trends, fashions, social acceptability, and fear of ostracization are powerful operators on human behavior and can be used very effectively to manipulate people. The *ad Populum* fallacy leads people astray by mistakenly equating the popular with the normal, true, and acceptable. This phenomenon (known as "social proof" by compliance professionals) helps explain such occurrences as the sudden mania for collecting small stuffed animals and the perennial fascination with best-selling books and records.

Democracies are especially susceptible to this tyranny of the majority appeal, because political issues are commonly decided by majority vote. But truth and morality are not determined by popular vote, and to accept ideas or behavior patterns only because they are common can result in nothing less than delusion and oppression. As Anatole France reminds us, "If fifty million people say a foolish thing, it is still a foolish thing."

The point is, then, that as you search the Web, you should be suspicious of arguments based largely upon their current popularity or the claim that "everyone" is in agreement. Be careful of phrases such as "best- selling," "popular," "America's favorite," "most people agree," and so on. Even Web page counters ("This site has been visited 74653 times since June 10") are basically subtle *ad Populum* appeals. The biggest danger of the *ad Populum* is that this "get with it" philosophy is really an appeal for you to throw away your mind and become a cork on the river of life, floating along without any motion or direction of your own. My advice is, don't just "go with the flow" unless the flow is going in the right direction.

Quoting Fairly Versus The Fallacy of Vicious Abstraction. If you are writing a research paper, you will be quoting from sources, and many sites on the Web quote other sources as well. Since quotation is by nature only a piece of an argument or statement, there is always the risk that the quotation will take on a meaning different from the one intended by the author–the meaning it had in the context of the entire argument. When such a change in meaning occurs, the Fallacy of Vicious Abstraction has been committed. In a word, this is the fallacy of misquotation. In its first form (quoting out of context) it is committed whenever a statement is removed from a context or discussion which is necessary for the statement's meaning. In the imaginary example below, notice how the quotation in the movie advertisement, while quoted accurately from the passage above it, takes on a different meaning, so that the original speaker seems to be saying something he never intended:

> Teenage exploitation films seem to be drawn from a pile of garbage that gets worse as time passes. There seems to be a contest to see who can make the most sickening, disgusting film ever. This one is the winner. It stands by itself. If you go to see it, be sure to take an air sickness bag. –Merv Chadford

> Merv Chadford says of the film, "This one is the winner. It stands by itself." –Movie Advertisement

A second form of the Fallacy of Vicious Abstraction occurs when a statement is quoted inaccurately–that is, some part of a statement is omitted, thereby changing the meaning of the statement, or the statement itself is changed somewhat. Note how different the original here is from its alleged sources:

> A little philosophy inclineth man's mind to atheism, but depth in philosophy bringeth men's minds about to religion. –Francis Bacon

> Bacon said, "Philosophy inclines men to atheism."

Paraphrases of opinions, stands, and even literary or philosophical works often contain vicious abstractions because the paraphrasers are not careful to include qualifications, details, exceptions, or circumstances that are essential to a proper meaning. For this reason, accurate conclusions can seldom be drawn from paraphrases.

Citing Sufficient Evidence Versus the Fallacy of Hasty Generalization. When you are arguing for a particular position, you want to cite evidence to support your conclusions. For a research paper of moderate size, you probably cannot cite every piece of evidence, but you should take care to cite enough so that your conclusions have adequate justification. If you are forming a conclusion from your research, be sure that you have enough sources to make the conclusion truly likely. The Fallacy of Hasty Generalization arises when a conclusion or generalization is made on the basis of too few instances or too little evidence. A reliable general truth or rule cannot be formed after observing one or two or three samples, because they may be exceptions rather than representative cases. It is especially risky to form a generalization based on a single Web source.

To avoid repeating a Hasty Generalization from a Web site, try to discover what kind of evidence your source used to form the conclusions it presents. (For cases where someone deliberately chooses unrepresentative examples to support an illegitimate conclusion, see Selection and Slanting, below.) To avoid creating your own Hasty Generalizations, be sure that you research your problem or question thoroughly and draw reasonable conclusions from the evidence you discover. Remember that generalizations tempered by such words as *tends, indicates, usually, seldom,* or *probably* are much more palatable than ones declaring *always, never,* or *every.*

Necessary Qualification Versus the Fallacy of Weasel Words. Few statements of truth are "always" or "never" the case. Most statements need some kind of qualification if they are to be accurate. Thus, we are used to reading information that includes qualifiers such as *usually, tends to, might,* or even *could help.* In most instances, these qualifiers are useful and even necessary. However, many

Critical Thinking Tip

In your own quoting, be careful to quote accurately, checking the spelling of all the words (especially names), and making sure that the meaning of the excerpt is substantially the same as the meaning of the passage you quoted it from. It is especially important to check for fairness when you use ellipsis to leave words out.

qualifiers can be used deceptively, with the result that what is a qualified statement appears not to be.

Some writers wish to make their assertions as impressive as possible, without being caught saying what is not really true. To "weasel" around this problem, a rhetorical trick has come into use whereby a rather intemperate claim can be made and then partly recalled or qualified through the use of one or more weasel words. These words serve as invisible qualifiers because the reader tends to ignore them in favor of the general sense of the statement. For example, when we are told, "Fruit juice can help to cure your cold completely," we hear the "cure completely" but not the "can help." Thus, the net effect of a weasel-worded statement is to make the hearer believe more than is actually expressed while technically protecting the asserter from a charge of falsehood.

Dozens of limiting adjectives, adverbs, verbs, and nouns can be used as weasels. In fact, almost any word denoting qualification can be used as a weasel. It is up to you, then, to use careful judgment when you read a qualified statement. Many times the qualifications are fair, clear, and useful. But sometimes, they are intended to deceive.

A few words are used with some frequency as weasels and ought to be discussed briefly.

1. *Like.* This word introduces a simile, or comparison, and does not imply identity of objects, features, qualities, or experience. A simile implies similarity and since similarity is a matter of opinion, no real likeness is expressed. Whether something "looks like new" or "tastes like chocolate" depends on who is doing the looking or tasting.

2. *Can.* In formal English "can" means "to be able to," but in colloquial usage it sometimes means "might." An ambiguity like this can be (might be? is able to be?) exploited in such claims as "can make you feel better" or "can contribute to a better America," or "can be the solution we are looking for." It is one of the most frequently used weasels

Critical Thinking Tip

Some words commonly used as weasel words include these: *like, similar, look of, appearance, almost, virtually, feel of, helps, style, nearly, made with.*

because it is one of the most powerful. Notice the overwhelming difference between "It does pay a thousand dollars" and "It can pay a thousand dollars."

3. *Helps* and *Contributes*. The effective presence of a certain factor, even to an infinitesimal degree, may be said to "help" or "contribute to" a certain end. The statement, "Gritty Motor Oil contributes to longer engine life," appears to imply a significant contribution, but the real effect may be minuscule.

"Help" is problematic in an additional way. The word can mean both "relieve," "promote," or "benefit" and merely "assist." Thus the claim, "This vitamin supplement helps cure your insomnia," may mean either "promotes the cure of insomnia" or "assists (some other, unidentified thing) in the cure of insomnia." Note too that these two meanings of "help" can be equivocated: "Is there no help for the problems we face? Yes, my new bill will help solve the problems."

Common Fallacies of Argument

Here are some logical fallacies commonly encountered in Web information.

Argumentum ad Hominem. Also known as the Appeal to Personal Ridicule, this fallacy is one of the most common fallacies found on Web sites and newsgroup postings whenever a controversial issue is under discussion. The *ad Hominem* appeal relies upon character assassination as a substitute for refutation of an opponent's argument. Of course, a fact is true or false quite independently of the education, reputation, or other beliefs of the arguer; yet a surprising number of disputants yield to the temptation to attack the ability or character of an opponent rather than to present cogent rebuttal arguments. Worse, the attack often amounts to nothing more than insult and invective. If an arguer resorts to using words such as *extremist, idiot, ignorant, stupid,* and the like, it may be because he or she cannot think of any serious, factual rebuttal to the opponent.

Always remember that an argument can be legitimately attacked only by another argument. Truth does not always dwell with our friends, the good, and the sober; it is therefore our duty to look beyond personality and examine fairly whatever assertions, evidences, or positions are put forward.

Suppressed Quantification. Among the several kinds of ambiguous statements that represent sloppy thinking, a particularly worrisome kind involves an unqualified plural, blurring the distinction between *some* and *all*. An example would be, "Economists say that this policy is unworkable." Does this mean that all economists are saying that? Most? Many? Some? A few? Two? In all probability only *some* or *a few* really are saying this, but the impression such an unqualified plural gives is almost invariably that of *all* or *almost all*. Notice that in assertions such as "Scientists fear that California will fall into the ocean if there is another earthquake," and "Americans really like sushi," we assume an *all* or at least a *most* in front of the collective noun, when in fact the asserter would likely admit to a meaning of *some* or *a few* if challenged.

This fallacy occurs quite commonly in everyday discourse, largely because it has become an ingrained habit of sloppy thinking, and partly because some people like to use it to deceive. So habituated are we to thinking and talking in unqualified plurals that this fallacy is often difficult to spot—we simply overlook it. Be on your guard, though, against this fallacy in material you read and avoid this mental carelessness in your own work.

The Fallacy of Accent. This fallacy arises when the meaning or significance of a true statement is distorted or changed because of improper emphasis upon a part of the statement or upon the whole statement. In its simplest form the fallacy occurs when the emphasis (accent) in a sentence is placed upon a particular word in such a way that the meaning is changed from the author's real intention. For example, the commandment, "You shall not covet your neighbor's wife," takes on quite a different apparent meaning if read as, "You shall not covet your *neighbor's* wife," because it then seems to imply that coveting the wife of a non-neighbor is all right.

The more serious and dangerous forms of the Fallacy of Accent involve the whole statement and create significant deception by overemphasizing literal truth. An arguer creates the distorted emphasis by carefully selecting, isolating, and presenting some fact or statement that automatically gains apparent significance simply because it has been brought into prominence. The arguer may then use the improperly or excessively emphasized truth as the basis for a seemingly reasonable conclusion. For example:

> In the United States, aspirin is responsible for more than 10,000 cases of poisoning a year, many so severe that medical experts say, "Death may result despite all recommended procedures." As little as 10 grams can be fatal, and much less than that can cause vertigo, delirium, vomiting, hallucinations, convulsions, and even coma. I think it is clear that we should outlaw aspirin.

More commonly an arguer will allow the hearers of a statement to draw their own conclusions from his statement. When a statement itself is absolutely true, but implies something false, or leads to a seemingly obvious conclusion which, however, is false, a form of the Fallacy of Accent is committed–*suggestio falsi* (false suggestion). For example, consider what seems to be implied by this statement: "The almonds in this candy bar contain arsenic." While the statement clearly appears to suggest that the almonds in this candy bar are exceptional (and poisonous), the fact is that all almonds, and many other foods, contain arsenic in trace amounts.

Another form of the Fallacy of Accent occurs when one true fact or statement is presented, while another important fact or circumstance is not presented. This is called *suppressio veri* (suppressing the truth). *Suppressio veri* can be very difficult to detect because the suppressed truth must be known in advance if it is to be recognized by its absence. Suppose, for instance, you read the following claim: "This cereal is fortified with eight essential, nutritious vitamins and minerals. Plus it's high in fiber and full of corn and wheat goodness." The claim sounds good until you learn that the cereal is also 53 percent sugar. The best way to prevent yourself from being victimized by this fallacy is to inform yourself about all sides of an issue, and about the pros and cons of each position or decision.

Emotive Language. The Fallacy of Emotive Language involves the use of words aimed at feelings instead of at reason. When certain words used in an argument have the purpose of stirring the emotions to block an opponent's reasoning ability, then the Fallacy of Emotive Language is committed. Many words have strong positive or negative connotations attached to them, and these words can make the hearer or reader tend to react to words instead of to the real issue behind them. The way around emotive language, of course, is to focus on the argument and not allow yourself to be distracted by words–however evocative or incendiary they may be.

It is important to note that not every use of emotionally loaded language is fallacious, for occasionally we feel strongly about an issue and want to show our joy or make our "righteous indignation" clear. The fallacy occurs when our intention is to persuade someone and when our language interferes with, colors, or substitutes for legitimate reasons.

Negative Emotive Language. In its simplest form, negative emotive language is simply name-calling. For example, the statement, "That plan is not only reactionary and extremist, but it's also simplistic," is not an argument but merely a collection of emotionally loaded words. In a slightly more sophisticated form, a deliberate use of metaphors or other images can be used to evoke negative feelings: "My opponent would have us descend to the frozen rigor of a bygone era."

Positive Emotive Language. In addition to the use of negative emoters, many arguers are fond of using words that have a positive force. Notice how easy it is to take a word standing for an ideal or concept we like and to attach it to some concept that the arguer wishes to recommend to us: "We demand free parking on campus as one of every student's basic, inalienable rights." Few people feel comfortable opposing anything that is claimed to involve freedom, liberation, rights, progress, justice, and so on. Many arguers successfully exploit these "purr words" (as they are sometimes called) to gather support for programs or candidates, even though the real issues are not made clear.

On its subtlest level emotive language can be used for emotional coloration in what might otherwise appear to be descriptive prose; the language can either convey the writer's attitudes—of approval or disapproval—or color, by emotive terms, certain objects or events. How a situation is characterized by a writer can have a significant effect upon our perceptions of and attitudes toward it.

Begging the Question. This fallacy occurs when the initially stated point to be proved is later used in the argument as an already accepted fact, to support some new point at issue. Thus the original statement is eventually used to prove itself true, and hence the other name for this fallacy, circular reasoning. Thesis A is supported by point B; point B is then supported by thesis A (now called fact A). Consider this example: "Many intelligent people believe in ghosts. This is clear because several intelligent people told me so. And I know they were intelligent because they all believed in ghosts."

Sometimes essentially the same assertion is changed into different words and used directly as "evidence" to prove itself as first given: "I think Jones is guilty. Why? Because I think he did it."

In another form of this fallacy, a definition is written so that it begs the question. In other words, it defines a term or phrase in such a way that, when used in an assertion, it proves the assertion true by the very way the term is defined. Any objection to the assertion is silenced by appealing to the definition. For instance, suppose an arguer says, "All properly informed people oppose mining ocean-floor mineral nodes." Then, anyone named to be in favor of such mining can be declared "not properly informed" by definition. Similarly, the statement, "Mainstream scientists reject the possibility of cold fusion," by definition relegates supporters of the idea to the fringe of science.

Selection and Slanting. Selection and slanting are two of the most common methods of presenting an unfair argument. Selection involves choosing only facts (or writers or studies) that support the arguer's position. By this method, it is easy for an arguer to imply

Critical Thinking Tip

Be cautious when you discover too many adjectives trying to push your opinion around. Let the facts or events influence your judgment.

that the position being presented has no opposition or at least that the weight of evidence is on the arguer's side. A refinement of the technique of selection is for the arguer to pretend to present two sides but to choose weak or ineffective representatives of the side the arguer opposes. (Such a technique is known as the Straw Man Fallacy, because the opponent is being set up and is knocked down easily.) Some writers avoid stating arguments against their position; they prefer that you hear only their side, because it is much more convincing that way. Remember that a one-sided view can be extremely convincing, even though it is totally false, or at least warped beyond any resemblance to reality.

Slanting is a technique for influencing the reader's perception of an argument through the careful choice of words and emphasis. Slanting may include the use of euphemisms to make something bad sound less bad ("I didn't lie; I misspoke"), or of coloring adjectives to diminish or enhance a noun ("my opponent's little plan"). The usual puffery seen in advertising and politics ("This major breakthrough of an important new idea") is an example of slanting at work. Indeed, slanting is a good job description for today's "spin doctors," whose task it is to cast events in a desired light by dressing them in carefully chosen words. For example, if they like a plan that saves money, it is "thrifty," and if not, it is "stingy."

✭ Chapter 8 ✭

Ethics in the Information Age

"On the Internet, no one knows you're a dog." —*New Yorker* cartoon

"In a medium where no one knows you're a dog, there's got to be something to keep you from acting like a snake." –Robert Hertzberg, Editor, *Internet World*

The Need for Ethics on the Web

When they think about the behavior often seen on the Web, many observers seem to conclude that "WWW" stands for the Wild West Web, a lawless wilderness where cybercowboys ride with unholstered mice, ready to click and run without remorse. However vivid such a picture may be, one thing is clear: the Web cannot flourish unless it is used according to some standard of fair conduct by both the content creators (those who put information on the Web) and content users (those who use the information from the Web). Here is a look at the reasoning supporting this conclusion.

Defining Ethics

Ethics refers to a code of conduct based on standards that everyone in a society can agree on. Codes of ethics are derived from the values of a society or culture, from its history, traditions, religious principles, or even common sense ideas about fair behavior. In the history of thought, the great philosophers (Aristotle, Plato, Cicero, Confucius, Mencius) have all held that the values that support modern ethical codes–truthfulness, integrity, fairness, justice, honesty– are the values that promote mutual happiness and prosperity. Being ethical, then, and encouraging others to do the same, is beneficial for the preservation of trust and hence communication and the reliability of the information on the Web.

The Web Is About Communication

Most people come to the Web to get information, share ideas, ask questions, or even engage in commercial transactions. This communication takes place between people who in most cases have never seen each other, but who are willing to believe in the truthfulness and reliability of each other in order to learn something or to further enhance their lives.

The Basis of Communication Is Trust

Relationships between people (which, some believe, form the basis of civilization) are based on trust. When someone declares an opinion, makes a promise, or states a fact, you must trust that the person is telling the truth and not trying to deceive or manipulate you. If you should begin to doubt that you can trust the other person, communication and the relationship will either be severely constrained or come to a halt altogether.

Trust Is Strengthened by Ethics

Especially on the Web, where you cannot see the person whose information you are using, and where you have no history of personal knowledge about a person, a belief that ethical behavior is the standard for the interactions and exchanges is crucial. For example, sales sites with reputations or policies for ethical behavior enable you to feel comfortable shopping on the Web, where you must give out your credit card information and your mailing address. Even if you are simply reading some information on a Web site, the assurance you feel about the credibility of the information—your trust in the site—will be increased by the knowledge that the site creators possess ethical standards. To use the Web with confidence, you must be able to trust the people at the other end of the wire.

Principles of Computer Ethics

If trust is to be developed among creators and users of information found on the World Wide Web, then it is necessary to develop a basic set of principles for using computers. Several organizations are currently working to develop such guidelines, among them the Center for Computing and Social Responsibility and the Computer Ethics Institute. The following principles are adapted, with permission, from the Ten Commandments of Computer Ethics by the Computer Ethics Institute.

1. Do not use a computer to harm other people.
2. Do not interfere with other people's computer work.
3. Do not snoop around in other people's computer files.
4. Do not use a computer to steal.
5. Do not use a computer to bear false witness.
6. Do not copy or use proprietary software for which you have not paid.
7. Do not use other people's computer resources without authorization or proper compensation.
8. Do not appropriate other people's intellectual output.
9. Think about the social consequences of the program you are writing or the system you are designing.
10. Always use a computer in ways that ensure consideration and respect for your fellow humans.

Let's look at these principles one at a time and discuss the implications each has for both organizational and personal behavior on the Web.

1. Do not use a computer to harm other people.
Organizational violations of this principle include hate sites (sites devoted to demeaning, insulting, or threatening others), rumor mongers (who are more interested in spreading scandal than truth), and sites that violate the privacy of others (by posting personal information, for example). This principle warns us to beware of creating the potential for harm inadvertently, as well. For example, some sites have posted employees' Social Security numbers on the Web, leaving those employees open to identity theft and the credit problems that may follow.

On a personal level, individuals violate this principle when they use the Web to harass others in a computer lab by displaying pornographic pictures or by leaving pictures of mutilated bodies or aborted fetuses on the screen when they leave. Pranksters who enter the names, personal information, or e-mail addresses of others to register them at Web sites without permission violate this principle, too, even if the Web site is seemingly harmless. None of us like to receive junk e-mail or unwanted attention from strangers.

This principle represents an important ethic because each of the violations mentioned above can be done thoughtlessly and yet can cause personal endangerment, economic loss, or psychological harm.

2. Do not interfere with other people's computer work. Hackers (people who break–hack or chop, in a figurative sense–into computers to cause harm) violate this principle by altering, damaging, or deleting information from Web sites. Some hackers mount false Web pages on the servers of others, as in the famous case involving the Department of Justice, where hackers replaced the government's Home Page with a "Department of Injustice" Home Page. Other hackers interfere with the sites of others by mounting denial of service attacks against Web servers. These attacks involve requesting so many pages so frequently that the server becomes overloaded and cannot respond to legitimate requests. Sometimes the servers even crash completely and must be repaired before they can be restored to service.

If the Web is to be the highest example of free speech, as Internet promoters sometimes claim, then that must mean allowing everyone's voice to be heard. Those who cripple or disable the sites of others are in effect arguing that free speech is selective and that the speech of their enemies can be silenced at will.

On a personal level, this principle is violated when the Web pages or files of others are altered or erased. Information sabotage is an unfortunate reality in a perhaps overly competitive educational world, but it is still wrong. Respect the files of others and others will be more likely to respect yours.

3. Do not snoop around in other people's computer files. Most of us have a desire for privacy in our lives: we want people to knock when we have the door closed, we do not want other people reading our mail, and we want our telephone conversations to be private. Others express their politeness and respect for us by honoring our desire for privacy in these areas. The same is true for privacy in cyberspace. The files that we create may contain personal information that we want to keep personal. And, by the Golden Rule of "Do unto others as you would have them do unto you," we should respect the privacy of the files of others. Whether those files contain personal diaries or merely notes for a research paper does not matter. The files of others should be considered off limits, as a matter of courtesy, unless we are given specific permission to look at them.

On the Web, this principle means that restricted areas should not be entered without permission. Some areas are reserved for members of a working group, for paying customers, or for registered users. Whatever the reason, you should not barge into their group or area uninvited.

4. Do not use a computer to steal. The growth of Web commerce has been phenomenal, with billions of dollars' worth of sales conducted each year online. Unfortunately, some unscrupulous people use the Web as a means to steal, setting up various kinds of scams, ranging from pyramid investment schemes to chain letters to phony stores. Criminals who may be too cowardly to look you in the eye and cheat you are more than willing to steal your money from a few thousand miles away. Just because you come upon a fancy and professional-looking Web site, do not automatically conclude that a reputable business is behind it. Your grandfather used to say, "You can't judge a book by its cover." Today we say, "You can't judge information by its Home Page."

On a personal level, stealing on the Web usually means stealing information. Plagiarism (copying another's words without proper acknowledgement) is a form of theft, as is the copying and distribution of the intellectual property of another, whether that property is text, music, video, or images. You should be on your ethical toes here, because copying is so easy that it hardly seems like stealing. (Computer time and access can be stolen as well: see principle 7 on p. 117.)

Ethics Tip

It may or may not be easy to circumvent a password-protected area. Ease of breaking in is not the issue. The saying, "Locks are to keep out honest people," reminds us that privacy devices like passwords are signals for us to keep away as a point of honor, not challenges to our ability to break in.

5. Do not use a computer to bear false witness. Today, most major cities have only one newspaper, or perhaps two. In the heyday of the newspaper, however, many major cities had half a dozen or even a dozen papers all competing for the attention of the reader. One of the effects of the competition was that the papers not only strove furiously to get the most news and get it first, but also often tended to exaggerate events, manufacture news, and copy each other's ideas. The Web is now in a similar position of competitiveness for readers, with the result that the drive to be first and most dramatic sometimes overwhelms the desire to be accurate. Truth is sometimes slow to arrive, while many Web surfers want information immediately.

Another pressure put on the ethics of truthfulness is the ease with which less than the truth can be created—with the help of the computer. A serious danger connected with rumors and falsehoods spread over the Web is that they take on a very real and credible appearance. Whispered gossip can be dismissed as idle chit chat, but a story on the Web, perhaps accompanied by photographs or charts, can appear quite convincing. The site itself, with its slick formatting, can appear solid and reliable. If the information is printed out, it takes on the additional appearance of tangible, documentary evidence. You may recall the sensation and embarrassment caused when a well-known journalist fell for a Web hoax that claimed that TWA Flight 800 was shot down by a missile.

Even "photographic proof" can be faked easily now and posted convincingly on a Web page. Software that can alter photographs is now available for remarkably low prices, and the temptation to "fix up" images to suit a message or impression is ever present. You may have read about the news magazine that wanted to run a photo of a particular family on its cover. Unfortunately, the mom had bad teeth. So the magazine touched up the photo and gave her good teeth. Another magazine took a photo of a famous couple sitting on the beach and electronically turned the head of the man to create the appearance that he was about to kiss the woman.

As with the violations of all the other principles here, think of the effect these practices have on our trust. If we cannot trust a photograph to show what was really there, if a photograph is now merely an interpretation or a comment on reality, then we can no longer trust photographs to show us the truth. Therefore, these practices of doctoring photographs should be opposed so that we can retain our trust in the reality that photographs have traditionally offered. As things stand now, we must exercise caution toward all photographs, and apply the same standards of evaluation toward them as we do toward other forms of information.

6. Do not copy or use proprietary software for which you have not paid. Crimes that are easy to commit scarcely seem like crimes, and probably no crime is easier than copying software. The good news is that the two most popular Web browsers are currently both free, and many of the most popular and useful plug-ins also have free versions. Thus are many saved from crime by an absence of temptation. Of course, it is also possible to find on the Web bootleg copies of commercial software that the manufacturers do not want given away. Some of this software even includes viruses at no extra charge. Even if this bootleg software is safe and perfect, though, this principle warns us to avoid it and to respect property laws.

7. Do not use other people's computer resources without authorization or proper compensation. Users who steal a password to gain unauthorized access to a site, or who share a password with their friends so that the friends do not have to pay for their own password, violate this principle. As we have said earlier, stealing is so easy in the land of computers that sometimes people do not recognize what they are doing. If passwords weighed forty pounds and people had to break into a storeroom to get one, fewer people would steal them, simply because it would be obvious that they were stealing. But since a password is just a string of letters and numbers that can be repeated or written down in seconds, the sense of unethical behavior is often missing.

The point is that intangible resources–intellectual property, computer time, software–are not any less property than physical resources. If we are to continue to encourage others to develop these resources, we must be sure that their creations are used legally.

8. Do not appropriate other people's intellectual output. Some Web sites violate this principle by pulling in the content of another site and then showing their own advertisements to the user. The use of frames to display a site's menu and advertising with another site's content is a typical example of this appropriation or, to be less euphemistic, theft.

On a personal level, this principle reminds us that even if we have permission to use someone else's information products, we are not entitled to call them our own. You may already have heard about the companies who are willing to sell you a term paper or even give you one free ("for research purposes only" they claim, even as they send it to you double spaced in a typewriter font). But when you copy others' information and claim authorship, whether you copy from a site, a bought paper, or a free paper, you are still plagiarizing, still cheating.

9. Think about the social consequences of the program you are writing or the system you are designing. The distribution

Ethics Tip

If you buy a term paper and turn it in as your own, you are actually paying someone to diminish your future career. How? The truth is, a college *degree* really has very little value. It opens only the first door to a job. A college *education* is the product that has real value. If you take shortcuts to your degree by buying your papers, you may get the door open to a first job, but you have not gained the education needed to perform. In the business world, failure to perform means failure to get promoted.

of information has social consequences. In the film industry forty years ago, a famous actor removed his shirt and revealed that he was not wearing an undershirt. This one scene nearly destroyed the undershirt industry almost overnight. During the same era, tobacco companies encouraged actors to smoke in films to encourage others to smoke by imitation. Web sites now offer the same potential to influence others. Tens of millions of people have access to the Web today, and many of them are impressionable young people. Therefore, if you are designing and mounting your own Web pages, it is incumbent upon you to think carefully and long about the potential effect your material may have.

10. Always use a computer in ways that ensure considera-tion and respect for your fellow humans. Suppose you are writing a paper on surgical techniques for repairing gunshot wounds. The sites you visit show details of operations. Knowing that some people are extremely squeamish at the site of blood or open wounds, it would be considerate of you to visit these sites at a computer away from others. Notice that this behavior is just common sense kindness, where you think about the welfare of others before you engage in some Web use that may be upsetting.

Similar cases of consideration and respect might include planning your public-lab Web surfing in such a way that you do not end up monopolizing a computer that is in high demand (let other users have some time online, too), not changing settings or storing your personal bookmarks on public-use systems, and conserving resources by printing only the most useful documents (and by saving to disk whenever possible).

Netiquette

The term netiquette refers to etiquette on the Internet. Etiquette refers to more than where to place the dinner fork; it relates to ethics because it, like ethics, involves the relationship of trust between people. Most of the rules of netiquette were developed as behavioral guidelines for e-mail and newsgroup postings, where writers sometimes forget how to be considerate. These rules may be useful for you as a Web user because you may wish to write to the creators of some of the sites you locate. Netiquette, then, includes the following principles:

★ Take extra care to be polite, since you are addressing a

stranger when you write to a Web site creator. Generally, the less you know someone, the more formal you should be, to avoid giving offense unintentionally.

★ Be very careful of humor, sarcasm, irony, or criticism. In face-to-face conversation our tone of voice, gestures, and facial expression all provide contexts of interpretation for our words, and these contexts help reveal our humorous or calm or gentle attitude. Because these contexts are missing in an e-mail, though, many comments are subject to misinterpretation.

★ Do not write repeatedly if you do not get a reply. A second e-mail is all right, because the first might not have arrived, but after that, assume that your correspondent is either not interested or on vacation.

★ Always sign your e-mail with your full name, and preferably a description of who you are. A signature file that contains your name, major, and educational institution will make you more human to your correspondent.

★ Do not use e-mail as a weapon to harass someone, to forward chain letters or hoaxes (see the next section), or to send hate letters.

Ethics Tip

Virginia Shea has posted her Netiquette book online at *www.albion.com/ netiquette/book/* and it provides much more information about this subject.

Hoaxes, Urban Legends, and Chain Letters

Hoaxes

Perhaps you have received an e-mail promising you $1,000 or $5,000 to forward an e-mail message to your friends, or perhaps the mail solemnly warned you against opening any mail with the subject of "Good Times," or "Pen Pal Greetings." Hoaxes like these are common on the Internet, because some people view information–or in this case, disinformation (see p. 124)–as a game. There have always been tellers of tall tales, of course, but now such tales can be disseminated rapidly via e-mail and Web sites. New users are especially susceptible to being fooled by an Internet hoax, because they do not have the experience or context to know what is likely to be true or false.

If you are wondering why hoaxes are considered an ethical issue rather than unobjectionable pranks, consider the Death Ray hoax. Suppose that you are a new computer user who still has a limited understanding of how computers work and what is possible for them to do. Suppose also that the following e-mail arrives in your mailbox one day:

> A deadly new computer virus that actually causes home computers to explode in a hellish blast of glass fragments and flame has injured at least 47 people since August 15, horrifying authorities who say millions of people are risking injury, blindness or death every time they sit down to work at their PC!

> "Computer viruses of the past could disable your computer, but this virus goes a step further–and can kill you," declared Martin Heriden, a computer expert who specializes in identifying computer viruses. "This virus doesn't carry the usual 'markers' that enable it to be detected. It slips through the cracks, so to speak.

> "It is an extremely complicated process. But suffice it to say that the virus affects the computer's hardware, creating conditions that lead to dangerous short circuits and power surges. The end result? Explosions– powerful explosions. And millions of Internet users are at risk."

> The virus, nicknamed Death Ray by experts like Heriden, surfaced in England on August 1. A 24-year-old college student was permanently blinded when his 15-inch color monitor exploded in his face.

> "So how do you protect yourself? I wish I knew," said Heriden. "You either stop using the Internet or you take your chances until we can get a handle on this thing and get rid of it for good."

It seems highly likely that you as a new user would be quite frightened by this message, possibly granting it enough credibility that you would stop using the Internet. Hoaxes like this are not just fun pranks–they are cruel.

Here is a list of some of the more common virus hoaxes. Please note that all of the following, like Death Ray, are false. If you read a message warning about a virus with any of the following names, ignore the message and do not forward it to "everyone on your mailing list."

> Good Times
> Penpal Greetings
> Returned Unable to Deliver
> Make Money Fast
> Join the Crew
> Win a Holiday
> AltaVista Londhouse
> Ghost.exe
> Deeyenda
> Naughty Robot
> Internet Cleanup Day
> Hacker Riot
> PKZ300

Whether you are a new or experienced user of the Web, you can find out about many of these hoaxes from other members of the Web community. If you receive a message warning of some danger and urging you to send it along, do a little research first. There are several sites that follow virus hoaxes and urban legends, reporting on the origin, scope, and truthfulness of each one. (They are almost always false.) Here are several sites you can use to check out a new, shocking, or unrealistic story that drops into your mailbox or displays on your browser. Bookmark these sites so you can find them easily.

For warnings about viruses:

> Department of Energy Computer Incident Advisory Capability
>   at *http://ciac.llnl.gov/ciac/CIACHoaxes.html*
> Computer Virus Myths page at
>   *http://kumite.com/myths*
> IBM's Hype Alert Web site at
>   *http://www.av.ibm.com/BreakingNews/HypeAlert*
> Symantec AntiVirus Research Center Hoax Page at
>   *http://www.symantec.com/avcenter/hoax.html*
> Network Associates Virus Hoax Listing at
>   *http://www.nai.com/services/support/hoax/hoax.asp*
> Dr. Solomon's Hoax Page at
>   *http://www.drsolomon.com/vircen/vanalyse/va005.html*
> Data Fellows Hoax Warnings at
>   *http://www.europe.datafellows.com/news/hoax.htm*

Urban Legends

Another category of information hoax is the urban legend. Urban legends are usually accounts of moral punishment, described either in events that supposedly just happened or as a warning that dire consequences may happen to you. You may have received an e-mail allegedly from a woman who was tricked into paying $250 for a cookie recipe. She is now getting revenge by distributing the recipe and asking everyone to forward it. Or you may have seen a warning about students and businessmen who leave a party with an attractive young woman only to have a drink, pass out, and awaken with a kidney stolen. A few urban legends had their beginnings in a kernel of truth that became distorted or got out of hand, but most are merely inventions—stories intended to fool the unsuspecting.

Most of the hoaxes and urban legends have three characteristics that allow them to be identified as false:

1. The message reports on some amazing or exciting event or danger that you have never before heard about. (For example, if kidneys were being stolen all over the country, wouldn't you expect to hear about it from a regular news source?)
2. The message contains details to make it appear credible, but which are seldom the kind of details that can be checked. For example, the Death Ray virus hoax message quoted above includes details such as the claim that the virus "surfaced in England on August 1." The victim is a "24-year-old college student" who was injured when a "15-inch color monitor" exploded. Note that the details give the warning a kind of journalistic flavor, a sense of realism, yet not one detail is the kind that can be researched and either verified or disproved. (Interestingly, as these hoaxes spread, they tend to gain details rather than lose them.)
3. The message usually urges the reader to "send this message to all your friends" as a means of perpetuating it.

Here are some sites that track and expose urban legends:

The Urban Legends Web Site at
  http://www.urbanlegends.com
Urban Legends Reference Pages at
  http://www.snopes.com
Mining Company Urban Legends Page at
  http://urbanlegends.miningco.com

Similarly, if you read about any of the following stories, do not believe their claims. All of these popular urban legends and chain letter e-mails are hoaxes:

$250 Neiman Marcus Cookie Recipe
American Cancer Society & Sick Children (Jessica Mydek, Anthony Parkin, "a little girl dying")
Mark of the Beast 666 in Barcodes
Stolen Kidneys
Hawaiian Good Luck Charm
PBS NPR Petition
Madalyn Murray O'Hair Petition RM 2493
Procter and Gamble and Satan
Gerber Baby Food Savings Bond
Bill Gates E-mail Tracing
Walt Disney Jr. E-mail Tracing
ATT 9-0-# Phone Scam

As you can see from these lists, even though they are not exhaustive, there are many pranksters and many more good-intentioned but gullible people all too eager to believe a Web page or forward a message containing a warning, compassionate plea, or promise of possible financial gain. Note that a forwarded message is not made more credible simply because it was sent to you by someone you know or respect, unless that person has actually investigated the message itself. (Some messages even contain a line claiming, "I called the company and this is legitimate," but, of course, that is just another element of the hoax. Be cautious. Be careful. Be thoughtful.

Chain Letters

Several kinds of chain letters exist on the Web and through e-mail. The first contains a hoax or urban legend like those described above. Most of these are merely nuisances, filling mailboxes with useless and wrong information. Even these seemingly innocuous pieces can be harmful, however, if they contain an innocent person's e-mail address (who then receives thousands of replies), or if they name an organization that then must fight the false story. For example, Gerber, Procter and Gamble, and the American Cancer Society all spend many hours of time and thousands of dollars responding to the groundless but persistent stories about them.

A second kind of chain letter is the traditional pyramid scheme. It may request that you send money, fabric squares, or some other item of value. These letters promise a huge payoff to participants, but the payoff never happens. In addition to being fraudulent and unethical, these letters are illegal. See the article on chain letters by the U.S. Postal Inspection Service at *www.usps.gov/websites/depart/inspect/chainlet.htm* for more information.

A third kind of chain letter asks only that you send it on as a "message of cheer and good news" or "to bring you love and luck." At best these letters are a waste of computer resources and personal time, and at worst they can be threatening and harassing. Some of them mention dire consequences (unemployment, divorce, death) if the letter is not forwarded.

Information Warfare

Information warfare might be defined as the art of using information as a weapon. Consider the following events that have recently taken place on the Web:

* ✮ A company spreads false rumors about a competitor in order to steal the competitor's customers
* ✮ A Web message board is filled with criticism of a particular company's management and operations, and as a result, that company's stock price declines markedly
* ✮ An increasingly popular speaker and writer on ethics, now a religious Jew, is deeply embarrassed when nude pictures of her, taken twenty years ago when she was an atheist, are posted on the Web

As you can see, information has power to cause harm—especially when it can be distributed instantly to millions of people world wide. A key ethical concern over information on the Web, then, relates to the impact that information may have on those who are its subject. Certainly you should not spread stories you know to be false, but as a thoughtful citizen of cyberspace, you should think about the consequences that all information can have, and be careful not to spread stories carelessly, just because they are exciting.

Disinformation

The term *disinformation* refers to wrong or misleading information that is known to be wrong or misleading by those who spread it, but that is spread intentionally, in order to deceive others. The Web, of course, contains quite a bit of *misinformation*—information that is wrong because of ignorance, carelessness, or confusion—but it also hosts an increasing amount of disinformation. The ethical problem is clear: if some information on the Web (or anywhere else) is intentionally misleading, how confident can you be in any information? Here we return to the trust issue with which we opened the discussion of ethics in this chapter. Information that cannot be trusted is more dangerous than no information at all, because information strongly affects the direction of our choices. Your best protection against disinformation is careful reading, research, and corroboration. Consult chapter 5 on evaluating Web sources for some guidelines for discovering the quality and reliability of Web information.

Planted Information

Planted information may be true, false, fair, or misleading, but its source is disguised or even omitted so that a conflict of interest or motive cannot be discerned by the receiver of the information. Anonymous rumors, for example, sometimes have their origin in planted stories. With Web page creation software so easy to use now, almost anyone can create a Web site that may appear to have no connection with the creator. The Web has become a fertile ground for swindlers of every kind. Someone interested in helping a new book sell well may plant several highly positive reviews (under different names) on Amazon.com, just as someone who dislikes the ideas might plant several highly negative reviews of the book.

In another example, one stock trader first circulated very positive rumors about a company, which drove the stock price up. He then "sold short" (the quite legal process of selling shares not yet actually owned) thousands of shares and then circulated very negative information about the company. When the stock price plummeted, he bought the thousands of shares at the low price just in time to deliver the ones he owed to the buyers at the high price. In this unethical maneuver, the trader made tens of thousands of dollars by planting a few rumors. The reason we know about this activity is that the trader was caught.

In its fullest extension, information warfare involves issues related to privacy, industrial and governmental espionage, cyber-terrorism (such as disabling computers), the spreading of viruses, and acts of extortion, stock manipulation, and on and on. Those who practice information warfare are engaged in a serious undertaking, often with millions of dollars at stake, so you should be on your toes to avoid becoming an unwitting participant in someone else's financial or political scheme. For further information on this subject, visit the Information Warfare Web site at *www.infowar.com*.

—⇒●⇐—

The Ethics of Linking

A final issue relating to the ethics of the Web concerns the meaning and propriety of links from one Web site to another. Consider these scenarios and the related issues:

✷ At the end of a newspaper's book review section, there is a link to an online bookstore where the reader can purchase the book just reviewed. Does the link (paid for by the bookstore) represent a conflict of interest for the online paper, and does the financial relationship put pressure on the paper to review books more positively than it otherwise might?

✷ A well-known and respected search engine offers a few news stories for its readers. The engine's home page also includes a link to an all-news site, with the description, "More News Here." Does the presence of this link imply an endorsement by the search engine company of the news site? Will the search engine company's positive reputation influence the reader to see the news site in a similarly positive way, making its stories appear more reliable and its commentaries persuasive?

✷ A Web magazine publishes an article about dangerous Web sites, mentioning sites that give instructions for bomb making. It provides links to some of these sites so that readers can see for themselves. Do these links encourage dangerous behavior? Does the presence of the link in connection with the article serve to justify visiting sites that the reader would otherwise avoid?

In response to these issues, the following comments may help frame the debate.

A Link Should Not Necessarily Be Viewed as an Endorsement. While a link represents an opportunity and even an encouragement to access other information, providing a link should not be taken to imply that the site recommends the information. The link may have been paid for as an advertisement or it may have been put there by the writer or editor as a public service. In magazine publishing, products in advertisements are not viewed as being endorsed by the magazine. Everyone knows that advertisements are paid for. The same concept should apply to links from banner or other advertisements on a Web page.

However, this also implies that the links should be clearly marked as advertisements. If you are reading a story on a financial site and see that the name of each company mentioned is a hyperlink, you cannot tell whether that link will take you to further information or to an advertisement for that company's products. If you click through to find an advertisement, it is probably merely a revenue source. (The issue remains whether many embedded advertisements in editorial content can exist without influencing the content. For example, will the company continue to pay for hyperlinking its name if mention of its name is accompanied by criticism?)

In situations where the links are not to advertisements but to other sites, remember that the free exchange of information is one of the hallmarks of the Web. The creators of many sites link to other sites they do not support philosophically, because these creators want others to have the full range of fact and opinion. For example, the site TalkOrigins (*www.talkorigins.org*) covers the Creation/Evolution debate. The owners of the site itself are evolutionists, but they have linked to many creationist sites as well–without implying any endorsement.

If you create your own Web pages, you might want to supply information about the links you put on your pages, to reveal your judgment of them. "Here is a great site with valuable information," or "This link is for your information only–I disclaim any endorsement" would make your views clear. (Be careful not to libel or insult others.)

Paid Links May Represent a Potential Conflict of Interest. The conflict of interest issue is not unique to the Web, however. Every information source (newspaper, magazine, television, film, music) can run into questions of objectivity and fairness whenever the product accepts advertising. If a hotel chain or an airline sponsors a travel site on the Web, we rush to ask the question, Will that site feel free to criticize the hotel's cleanliness or the airline's pricing structure? But then, when the same hotel or airline runs full-page advertisements in the travel section of the Sunday paper, should we not ask the same question? The issue of advertising pressure on editorial content is a fundamental one of the information society. Most creators of editorial content are vehement in asserting that they are untainted by advertising pressures. Some even argue that the content is created before the advertising is sold, thus keeping content free of influence. However that may be, this issue needs ongoing consideration and debate.

Chapter 9

Using WebQuester Course-Specific Titles

For Instructors Only—What Is WebQuester?

This book and its interactive exercises provide an introduction to Web-based research. WebQuester course-specific titles incorporate the skills and techniques acquired here into the work required to complete the modules.

WebQuester course-specific titles are independent of any particular textbook. They provide a carefully selected series of Web sites focusing on the material expected to be discussed in a course and assessment based on those sites. While WebQuester gives students access to the most current information available in their course of study, it also gives them valuable experience using the resources of the World Wide Web. Students need only minimal computer skills to do WebQuester exercises; they are largely of the "point and click" type.

WebQuester consists of two things: an online component as its primary focus, and a brief book that discusses topics designed to help students not only work online, but also approach the material in an intelligent and critical way. The book also provides each student with an individual registration number. It is essential that each student use this number to register for the class online; it allows that student to appear on the instructor's roster and get credit for the work. At the end of the course the registration number expires and the student can no longer access WebQuester.

Features

The WebQuester format is standardized across all WebQuester titles. Each title contains the following:

★ Twenty topics that are traditionally covered within the course area.

✶ For each topic, three to four Web sites whose content supports the topic through examples, applications, further discussion, or a special angle. These sites are monitored regularly to ensure they remain viable and relevant.

✶ One to three multiple-choice questions per Web site (automatically graded by WebQuester).

✶ Two or three short-answer questions per topic.

✶ One to three essay questions per topic.

✶ Additional links are provided with each WebQuester as a resource for further study. The links are organized by general topics covered in the course of study.

✶ The student guide, *A Guidebook to the Web,* is a brief book that provides practical information and tips about such topics as: Searching the Web, Evaluating Information, Thinking Critically in a World of Information, and Computer Ethics.

✶ The Web Research Exercise is a perfect introductory module to every title. This online exercise is provided to accompany the material in the student guide and gives students an opportunity to practice finding their way around the Web, and to assess the quality and relevance of the material they find there.

✶ Each WebQuester title contains additional interactive exercises that are appropriate for that particular title. This may take the form of a glossary, interactive features, experiments, or Web surveys.

WebQuester as an Academic Resource

One of the advantages of the Internet is the range of choice of information it allows the user. It is this strength that allows the exercises to be used with various levels of undergraduate students. The authors of WebQuester have identified links to Web sites that are not only interesting and inviting, but also provide the most current information available for a given topic. The questions related to the sites should help students read with efficiency and purpose while at the same time provide the instructor with a practical means of assessing the work a student has done. More advanced students will find opportunities to investigate the topic further by following the links provided from the various Web sites themselves, or by utilizing the links listed under "Other Excursions" on the WebQuester home page. These sites were selected primarily for the fact that they contain some general information on the subject or the topic, and also because they contain many sources or links to other relevant sites.

All sites were selected strictly for their intellectual content; no author of any site has contracted with the publisher or the authors of WebQuester for reference in this product.

Students and instructors new to the world of the Internet and using technology in their courses will find that the guide has comprehensive information that will greatly facilitate their ability to surf, to find, and to assess knowledgeably what they do find.

Instructors: How to Order WebQuester

Step 1. Connect to WebQuester

★ Access the Internet.
★ Type in the following URL:
   http://www.dushkin.com/webquester/

Step 2. Sample WebQuester

★ Click on *Preview a WebQuester Title*.
★ Click on the arrow in the drop-down box and select the WebQuester you would like to examine for possible adoption.
★ Select one of the hyperlinked topics.
★ Enter at least one of the Web sites, and fill in some of the answer boxes.
★ At the end of the exercise, click on *Submit* to see how the program automatically grades the multiple-choice exercise and returns the score to the student. When your students have registered, you will be able to access their scores through the Professor Home Page. By clicking on the student's score for a particular module you can see and grade the short answer/essay question and e-mail that score back to the student.

Step 3. Order the Booklet

★ Place an order with your bookstore for the number of books you will need, corresponding to the enrollment for the course. Each student will need a book, since the unique keyword needed to register for the course is found inside the cover.

Step 4. Register for WebQuester Online

⋆ Click on *Order WebQuester* on the Home Page.
⋆ Fill out the form online; this sets up the system whereby students can select your class when they register online.

Instructor Support

Once you have ordered the book and registered online for your students, you will be directed to the Faculty Home Page that is password-protected for the faculty member alone. There are several options available from this page.

Access a WebQuester Student Site–Each of the WebQuester student sites is available from this page. They may be selected from the pull-down menu and are fully operational. By accessing the modules (topics) available for a particular course, you can begin planning the course outline and scheduling of modules.

Class Roster–This roster will show all of the students who have registered for a given course and will post their grades. WebQuester automatically grades the multiple-choice questions, but not the short-answer/essay. By clicking on the student's scores for a completed module, the student's responses to the short-answer/essay questions will appear. You should grade these online and e-mail the score back to the student, or print out the student responses, and grade them the traditional way and hand them out in class. In addition, by clicking on the student's name, you will have access to the student's Username and Password in the event that a student has forgotten it. If a student wishes to repeat a particular quiz, and you agree to it, you have the ability to reset the test for the student. The program will NOT perform this function automatically. (The specific directions are available online.) Students should be aware that once they have finished and submitted a module, it will not be available for retaking unless they first discuss the matter with you. This safeguard obviously prevents students from sharing answers and constantly changing what they have submitted.

Toolbox–This page contains options that will help you manage your course. You can look up a student's Username and Password, or reset any student's test so they can retake it. If you choose to use WebQuester for another semester, you can remove a current course, add a new course, or delete the users from a course and keep the title and section. This enables you to use WebQuester for another class without having to reregister. (Note: students still need to purchase a book and register for a new class in order to ensure that their names are associated with the correct class and instructor).

Instructor's Manual–From the Instructor Home Page, you will find detailed information on the format and content of the questions used in WebQuester, and descriptions of the other activities that are included in their particular subject. These activities may include glossaries, maps, figures, tables, or interactive exercises. Each of these additional materials is selected to enhance the particular subject matter of a specific WebQuester and not all of them will apply to all WebQuesters.

We hope you and your students enjoy using WebQuester. We're always looking for feedback on ways to improve the product. You can e-mail us from the Home Page with your suggestions.

For Students Only

What have you gotten into? Don't know a mouse from a moose? Don't know a URL from the Ural Mountains? Think a Web is the diabolical invention of sticky eight-legged creatures? Never fear! Welcome to WebQuester. This new and innovative way of doing research, keeping up with the latest information in your course, and working out course exercises online will give you a greater appreciation for the all the information available on the World Wide Web. If your professor has decided to assign a course-specific WebQuester title for your class, you will need to purchase, for a small additional fee, a registration number for that class. That number is found on the inside cover of the WebQuester course-specific guidebook and may also be available online.

Having read the material in this guidebook and completed the online activities that accompany each chapter here, you should be well-prepared to do the course-specific WebQuester exercises.

First you need to register online so that your name will appear on your instructor's class roster and so that your grade for each module will be registered there too. Follow the directions carefully so that you can complete the registration process easily.

How to Register for WebQuester

Step 1. Connect to WebQuester

✶ Start your Web browser and make a connection to the Internet.
✶ Type in the following Web address (the URL):
http://www.dushkin.com/webquester/

This will take you the Home Page of WebQuester. It should look similar to the one shown in Figure 1 below.

✶ Figure 1 ✶

Step 2. How to Enter WebQuester for the First Time

✶ If this is your FIRST visit to WebQuester, click your mouse on *Registration Page*. You should see an image that looks similar to the one displayed in Figure 2. You will need to register your keyword (found inside the cover of your course-specific WebQuester book) following the procedures listed below:
✶ Click your mouse in the "First and Last Name" textbox and type in your first and last names as they appear in your school registration materials.

⭑ Figure 2 ⭑

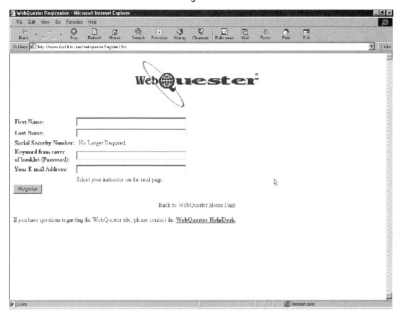

⭑ Click your mouse in the "Keyword" textbox and type in the keyword from this book.

⭑ Click your mouse in the "E-mail Address" textbox and type in your e-mail address. If you will be using a school machine and aren't sure of the e-mail address at that machine, ask your instructor. Since your grades will be sent to the e-mail address you enter, it is important that you get it right.

⭑ Click your mouse on "Register" and your browser will display a box in which your Username will appear. Be sure to record this Username because you will use it (and a Password you select) every time you enter WebQuester.

⭑ Choose a Password that will be unique to you. Click your mouse in the textbox marked "Password" and type in the Password you have selected. As a security check, you are asked to type it again. This Password is assigned only to you so that only you will be given credit for having completed the exercises. It is safest to choose a Password of at least six letters and numbers. Choose something that is not in the dictionary, but that has personal meaning for you. For example, if the last two digits of your mother's phone number are 82, you might choose the password *aidee2*. If you

WebQuester Tip

It's a good idea to write down your Username and Password in a safe place so you won't forget them; you will use them every time you enter WebQuester. You may want to record your Username and Password here.

Username

_____

Password

_____

Be sure not to lend or lose your WebQuester book! **Note:** Your keyword, username, and password are case sensitive.

had a pet named *Fuzzix,* you might choose *Fuzz6mo.* **Note:** The keyword you were assigned in the book will no longer be used, and cannot be assigned to anyone else. At the end of the semester, your Username and Password will no longer be valid and you will not be able to use WebQuester again. If you need to take an incomplete, or for some reason need to extend your usage beyond the end of the semester, please notify your instructor and she will be able to make an adjustment for you.

✷ Click on *Enter WebQuester.* You should see a page similar to that in Figure 3.

Step 3. How to Enter WebQuester When Previously Registered

✷ Be sure you scroll down the page far enough to see the section "Student Entrance." Click your mouse on the Student Entrance. This will take you to the Student Home Page.

✷ Select the course you registered for and click on it.

✷ Enter your Username that you were assigned and the Password that you selected.

✷ Click on "OK" and your browser should display an image that looks similar to the one shown in Figure 3. If you have trouble connecting, see your computer lab assistant or your instructor for help.

How to Navigate the WebQuester Site

After entering your Username and Password, you will be able to move easily among the major components of the site. Simply click on the icon on the left of the Home Page to go to the component you want. The components are described briefly below.

 Main Exercises—Here you will find a list of topics to be covered. Your instructor will let you know which of the modules you should be completing.

✶ Figure 3 ✶

![WebQuester: Criminology Home - Microsoft Internet Explorer]

Main Exercises

Other Excursions

E-mail Your Prof.

Help

Web Quester™
Criminal Justice

Written and compiled by
Raymond A. Eve
Dept. of Sociology and Anthropology
University of Texas, Arlington
and
Caryl L. Segal
Dept. of Criminal Justice
University of Texas, Arlington

Welcome

Interest in Criminal Justice often stems from a personal interest in looking at our systems for dealing with crime, identifying the best parts of the process, and working positively for change in those areas that need improvement. *WebQuester: Criminal Justice* attempts to provide a forum for this examination. It explores the systems that deal with crime in our society first hand, from policing and deterrents to punishment and sentencing. Some modules look at the interrelationship of varying interests within these systems. WebQuester achieves a balance of readings between the nature of crime, its increasing association with young people, the police, law, and the judiciary. The Web sites that the title examines are a combination of original source material and data as well as perspectives from participants in the systems themselves.

This title will become a source tool for your entire course of study.

Other Excursions–Here you will find a general list of reference sources or links to other sites on the World Wide Web in your subject area. You may find these helpful in doing research, in writing a paper, or in finding additional information about a topic.

E-mail–If you need a question answered, or help on some aspect of doing the work online, here is where you can find your professor's e-mail address.

Help–Click here if you need technical assistance from the WebQuester webmaster. You will also find a list of Frequently Asked Questions (FAQs) about the WebQuester product. You may find the answer to your problem here. We would suggest reading these FAQs before you start working on your exercises in any case.

Home–This page introduces you to the WebQuester, gives you author information, and provides access to the various components.

✷ Figure 4 ✷

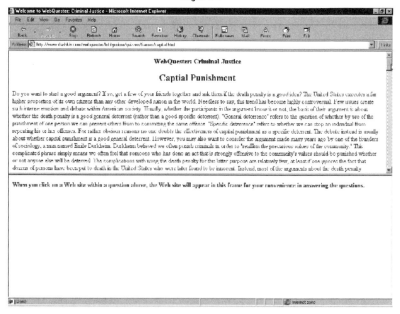

Step 4. How to Begin an Exercise

✷ Click your mouse on the "Exercises" button on the Home Page.

✷ Click your mouse on the topic of your choice, or the topic your instructor has selected. Your screen will now be divided into two frames or panels that will look similar to those displayed in Figure 4.

Step 5. How to Complete an Exercise

✷ The top frame of your screen will contain an introduction to the topic covered in that module. It provides valuable information about the topic and helps focus your attention on the material. Read this material first.

✷ Scroll down as you read and you will come to the first hyperlinked site and the questions to be answered. Click on the site and it will appear in the bottom frame of your screen. This allows you to read the material while the questions remain in the top frame, making it easier for you to focus on the information you want to find. If the site fails to appear, try again later. It may have a technical problem, or like a busy phone signal, it may have too many visitors at

the time you're trying to access the site. If the problem continues, please e-mail the WebQuester Help Desk. Include the specific WebQuester you're using, the name of the module, and the Web site that is giving you a problem.

★ Answer the multiple-choice questions that accompany the Web site link by clicking your mouse in the checkbox corresponding to the best response.

★ When you have visited each linked Web site and answered each of the multiple-choice questions, provide answers to the short answer/essay questions by clicking your mouse in the text boxes that follow the questions and typing in your answers.

★ When you have answered each of the questions, click the "Submit" button. Your score for the multiple-choice questions will be generated by the WebQuester computer and sent to you and your instructor. Your instructor will also have access to your short answer/essay questions and will evaluate them and e-mail you your grades. That's it!

WebQuester Tip

You may find it easier to read each frame by enlarging either the top or bottom frame. Point your mouse on the dividing line between the frames. When you see two arrows, hold the mouse down and just move the line up or down. When you're finished reading the material you can move the line back to its original position.

WebQuester Tip

Throughout the module you will find terms that are hyperlinked (underlined). If you click on these terms, you will find their definitions.

Student Support

Using WebQuester should be a fun and enlightening experience. However, as with anything new, you should make yourself familiar with utilizing the World Wide Web and with WebQuester before you begin to work. Those who know the Internet and the World Wide Web know the wealth of information that can be found there as well as the confusing kinds of information. WebQuester is designed to help you sort it out first by carefully selecting the kinds of sites that will give you the latest information

WebQuester Tip

All hyperlinked sites used in WebQuester are listed by a general topic title and by their URL or Web address. By looking carefully at this URL you can determine a site's domain name and from that determine whether the site is government, organizational, commercial, or military. Please see chapter 2, page 9 of *A Guidebook to the Web* for a detailed explanation of domain names.

in your subject area or that directs you to the kind of historical or background information that enhances the course material in a way that no textbook ever could. Secondly, the WebQuester book, *A Guidebook to the Web,* gives you an in-depth approach to critically analyzing and assessing the material you find on the World Wide Web as well as some practical guidelines and methods for finding information and citing whatever you might want to use in papers or reports. It can be a handy reference as well to topics such as Boolean Searches or Logical Fallacies in Thinking.

Frequently Asked Questions (FAQs) In the event you have difficulty accessing a Web site, forget your Username or Password, or experience other problems, a troubleshooting guide is available online from your course home page under the HELP logo. Your instructor may also be able to help you solve a problem, access a forgotten Username/ Password, or give you additional information on using WebQuester. If all else fails, please e-mail the WebQuester Help Desk by going to the HELP logo on the course Home Page.

Glossary

This glossary covers many of the terms related to using a Web browser to search the Web. If the term you need is not listed here, you might check Whatis?com at *www.whatis.com/nfindex.htm* for a much more extensive computer-related dictionary.

address. The collection of characters (the **URL**) that identifies a Web page or site so that a user can access the information.

ASCII. American Standard Code for Information Interchange. The code of digital ones and zeroes that represent the alphanumeric (letters and numbers) characters of the keyboard. Extended ASCII includes some simple graphic characters as well. An ASCII file is the same as a plain **text file.**

back. A button on a Web **browser** that takes the user to the previously displayed page. Clicking the mouse on the button repeatedly steps back sequentially though several previously displayed pages.

bookmark. A saved URL in a bookmark file. Bookmarks allow you to return to frequently visited sites or sites you want to visit again, without needing to type in the URL by hand. Very long URLs can be saved easily with the "Add Bookmark" command.

Boolean logic. A set of logical operators that allow control over the breadth of a search when two or more terms are used. The most common operators are AND, OR, and NOT. Two words joined by AND restrict a search (requiring that both terms be present for a successful hit), while two terms joined by OR expand a search (requiring that only one term be present for a successful hit).

browser. A program that allows you to access information on the Internet, especially on the Web. Technically, it is an application software program, functioning as a client to a remote host (the Web server). Netscape Navigator and Microsoft's Internet Explorer are the two most common browsers.

CGI. Common Gateway Interface. A system that allows a browser to become interactive with a host through the use of CGI scripts–short programs loaded from the host into the browser that allow filling out of forms, check boxes, and the like. CGI scripts can be written in any of several programming languages (such as C++ or Perl) and are often stored in a host directory named *cgi-bin*.

client. A computer or its software that requests information (such as Web pages) or operations (such as running a program) from a **host,** called a server. This design for computing is called client-server architecture.

cyberspace. The online world of information, especially the Internet.

default. A predetermined standard setting that will be used unless the user selects something different. In a word processor, for example, margins will be set by default at, say, one inch on each side unless the user wishes different margins. Nearly all application software has default settings until a user changes or customizes the program. On a Web site, the default page that will be sent when a site is requested without naming a specific page is called the home page. The default home page's file name is often *index.htm* or *default.htm*.

dialog box. A small window that appears (or pops up) on a computer screen and ask you to confirm an action, make a choice, change a setting, or perform some other activity.

directory. (1) A hierarchical subject guide of sites chosen by the editors of a search tool site or recommended to them. (2) A list of names and addresses, phone numbers, e-mail addresses, or businesses, often searchable by keyword. (3) A designated area on a hard drive where related files are stored. Also called a folder.

directory path. A series of directories and subdirectories that together identify the exact location of a file or final subdirecrtory. Many URLs include a directory path in addition to the domain name, as in *www.abc.com/first/second/third/file.htm*.

DNS. Domain Name Server. A computer that translates the numbers and letters of domain names (such as *www.vanguard.edu*) into their numeric equivalents, such as 206.215.36.2. Since humans like names and computers like numbers, the Domain Name system allows both to be happy.

domain name. The unique name of a Web server and its category (such as *.edu*). The shortest domain name has two words, as in news.com. The domain name is translated by a domain name server into the numerical address that the Internet actually uses to send information.

download. The action of transferring information from another computer to the user's computer. Whenever you save a Web file, image, or sound, you are downloading the file. Compare **upload.**

e-mail. Electronic mail, that is, mail sent in digital form rather than in print-ed, physical form. Printed mail, especially when sent through the post office, is sometimes called snail mail.

Error 404: Not Found. A requested file cannot be found on the host com-puter. You may have mistyped the **URL** or the file may have been removed.

ethics. A code of conduct based on standards that everyone in a society can agree on. Codes of ethics are derived from the values of a society or cul-ture, from its history, traditions, religious principles, or even common sense ideas about fair behavior. Web ethics is mostly common sense about politeness, consideration for others, fairness, and integrity.

FAQ. Frequently Asked Questions. A list of common questions and answers relating to a site or subject. Pronounced *fack*.

forward. A button on a Web **browser** that takes the user to the next page to be viewed in a sequence of viewed pages. The forward button will become available only after the **back** button has been clicked on one or more times with the mouse.

frame. A segment of a browser window. Frames are created by some Web page designers who wish to show some information in one section of the screen while replacing information in other sections. One section might contain a menu or an advertisement, while another will have text, for example. The collection of frames displayed at one time in your browser is called a frameset.

FTP. File Transfer Protocol. A method of sharing files among computers from remote locations. FTP can be used either to **upload** files or to **download** them.

GIF. Graphics Interchange Format. A method of compressing an image to save space. This is one of the two most common image formats on the Web. There are several versions in addition to the standard GIF. One is the interlaced GIF, which loads gradually, giving an overall but blurred image at first, and then gradually increasing in resolution. Another is the animated GIF, which is actually a series of several images which display in quick sequence, giving the appearance of movement. Pronounced *jiff*.

Gopher. An early menu-based system for choosing files to **download** from a **host.**

history file. A file that contains the URL of each page visited by a browser. History files can be set to expire after a certain number of days, so that only the most recent Web activity is retained. (For example, a history file with a ten-day expiration will keep only URLs that are ten days old or less. The history file is usually accessible as a clickable menu so that you can quickly return to any of the sites you have recently visited.

hit. An item returned by a search engine as the result of a search. ("I searched for information on Monarch butterflies and got 3,000 hits.") A hit also refers to Web page requests on a server. ("Our site is getting 20,000 hits a month.")

home. A button on a Web browser that returns the user to the **default** page set in the browser. The default page can be changed in the browser's settings. Netscape Navigator and Microsoft Internet Explorer default to each company's sites if the user does not change the preferred home setting.

home page. The default or first page displayed when you access a Web site without specifying a particular file name. This is the main page of the individual or organization.

host computer. A computer that answers requests for information from other computers. Also known as a server, the host computer "serves" up files, programs, or processes upon request of the **client** (asking) computer. On the Web, host computers are contacted by using the appropriate address or **URL.**

hotlist. Another name for bookmark list.

HTML. Hypertext Markup Language. A set of tags (markers) and codes that allow text, images, sounds, and video to be displayed on the Web, and to be linked together. The tags are placed within angle brackets. For example, the tag <img src = "pic.gif"> tells a browser to load an image file named "pic.gif" at the location of the tag. The tag <B> tells a browser to display the following text in boldface until the turn-off bold tag of </B> appears.

HTTP. Hypertext Transfer Protocol. A protocol (set of rules or procedures) that allow server host software to send and browser client software to receive Web documents.

hyperlink. An embedded address on a Web page that allows an automatic connection to another page simply by clicking the mouse on it.

hypermedia. A document or collection of documents containing hyperlinks not only to text files but to graphics, sound, and video. Hypermedia refers to the multimedia form of hypertext.

hypertext. A document or collection of documents containing hyperlinks, which allow a reader to jump quickly from page to page by clicking on the links.

image. A photograph, drawing, graph, map, or other pictorial element included in a Web page. Images can be saved by themselves by right clicking on them in Windows or clicking and holding with a Macintosh, and then choosing "Save Image As."

Internet. The global network of computer networks that allows information to be shared among all users through the use of various methods (called **protocols**), with the World Wide Web being the most popular.

JPEG. Joint Picture Experts Group. A graphic image format, with the extension .jpg, that allows for the image to be compressed into a smaller size for faster transfer over the Web. Because it can support many colors while maintaining a reasonable file size, JPEG is used most often for photographs, while GIF is used for graphics with only a few colors.

keyword. A word you want to search for in a document. One or more keywords are entered into the search box of the engine you are using.

link. A **hyperlink,** the word or phrase in a document that leads to another page, site, or location.

metainformation. Information about information. Metainformation comes in two forms, summary (such as an abstract) and evaluative (such as a review). Metainformation can be very useful as an aid in managing the glut of information on the Web and elsewhere.

mirror site. A site that has a duplicate copy of all the pages on another Web site. Mirror sites are created to take the load off an original site. Sometimes they are spread out geographically so that users can access a server nearer to them than the original site.

netiquette. A code of conduct encouraging polite, fair, and trustworthy behavior on the Internet. (Formed from a combination of *net* and *etiquette*.)

NNTP. Network News Transfer Protocol. A method used by Internet newsgroups for posting and reading bulletin-board style messages.

offline. Not connected to a network or the Internet. You may be using a word processing program while you are offline, but then wish to go **online** to access some information.

online. Connected to a network or the Internet, such as when you are using the Web or sending e-mail.

page. A collection of text and graphics (and sometimes audio or video) that loads together into a Web browser as a result of a single URL request. This definition may sound complicated, but a single Web "page" may actually be many screens long and require many paper pages to print out. It may also include pictures, tables, and even interactive forms.

password. An individual code that allows a user access to computer resources. Your password should remain confidential so that your files will be private and so that no one else can use the computer in your name. Passwords should be at least six characters long and include both letters and numbers, as in G6DL53R. If you do use a word, it should preferably be a nonsense or unique word not found in a dictionary (since some computer programs have been written to mount "dictionary attacks" that substitute every word in the dictionary, one after the other, as a means of breaking into a system).

plug-in. A helper program that enables a browser to display, play, or print information. Once a plug-in is installed, it will run automatically whenever needed. Common plug-ins include Acrobat Reader for printing and Real Player for playing audio and video.

portal. A Web site that offers a gateway to many areas of the Web, often including search capability, shopping, e-mail, news, software, book and music sales, games, and various directories (such as telephone or business).

protocol. A set of standardized settings, rules, or methods by which two computers (or other data devices, like fax machines) can exchange information. If you have ever heard the screechy, warbling, high-pitched tones that fax machines or computer modems make when they are connecting to each other, you have actually overheard a protocol discussion and agreement, known as handshaking. Web protocols include **HTTP** and **FTP,** while the Internet itself operates on a protocol called **TCP/IP.**

reload. A command (from button or menu) to a browser to request a Web page again from a host computer. If a page stalls while loading, sometimes choosing "Stop," and then "Reload," will bring the entire page in more quickly.

robot. See **spider.**

scrolling. The act of moving up and down through a long page in order to view it on a screen. Many pages require scrolling through several screens in order to view them entirely. Scrolling can be accomplished by using the mouse on the scroll bar (to the right of the screen), by using the "Page Up" and "Page Down" keys, or by using the up and down arrows on the keyboard.

search engine. A computer and software combination that indexes Web pages and permits users to search through the index to find Web sites of interest.

search tool. Any of several means for locating information. On the Web, search tools include search engines, subject **directories,** and specialty directories.

server. A host. Servers "serve" clients by sending information or performing other tasks. A Web server sends out Web pages upon request of the client. A mail server processes e-mail, and a print server handles print requests over a network.

site. A group of pages collected together around a main page. A single site is usually the creation of a single organization. However, a site may have several creators, but the content belongs together somehow, usually by subject.

SMTP. Simple Mail Transfer Protocol. A method used by many e-mail servers to receive and forward e-mail.

spam. Junk or otherwise unwanted information, sent without request. Junk e-mail such as sales promotions, chain letters, and pyramid schemes are examples of spam.

spider. A software program that accesses, reads, and indexes Web pages for a search engine. Spiders are also called robots or bots. The word is sometimes used as a verb, as in, "Has your page been spidered yet?"

stop. A button on a Web browser that terminates loading of a Web page. If you change your mind about viewing a page or if a page is taking too long to load, you can stop the loading and choose something else.

streaming. Arriving as it is played. Streaming audio and video files are not saved to disk before (or even after) being played, but arrive in a constant stream and are played as they arrive. The benefit is that the large amounts of data necessary for high quality can be sent without overwhelming the storage resources of the personal computer.

surfing. In the jargon of the Web, to move around on the Web, going from site to site. Another metaphor is navigating (note Netscape's product, Navigator).

TCP/IP. Transmission Control Protocol/Internet Protocol. The set of **protocols** that enables information to travel over the Internet. The protocols include those necessary for addressing and delivering Web pages and e-mail.

Telnet (from *tele,* distance, and *net,* network). A method for remotely logging onto a host computer, operating it as if from a nearby terminal connected directly to the host. A telnet client program causes a personal computer to emulate a host terminal, so that the host computer sees it as a terminal rather than as a computer.

text file. A file stored in "plain text" form, meaning in the ASCII standard, without any special codes or markup tags. Plain text files can be read by virtually every application program, from word processors to spreadsheets to browsers. The file extension *.txt* indicates a plain text file.

top-level domain. The two or three letter part of a URL that indicates the type of Web site, such as *.com* for commercial, *.edu* for educational, and *.org* for organization.

urban legend. A fascinating but usually fictional story spread over time throughout a culture, often detailing gruesome punishments for indiscreet actions. Urban legends are told as true, with the claim that they happened recently to "a friend of a friend." With the advent of the Internet, these stories are spreading faster than ever.

URL. Uniform Resource Locator. An address, usually in name form, for something on the Internet. Every page on the Web has a unique URL.

virus. A self-copying computer program that attaches itself to other programs and infects computer files when the programs are used. Many viruses cause some kind of harm to the infected computer, such as erasing the hard drive or damaging files. Virus programs are deliberately written by malicious programmers; they do not occur by accident. The best preventative against viruses is to use anti-virus software, which can detect and remove viruses.

Web ring. A collection of Web sites covering the same subject or theme and connected together by organized hyperlinks. Each site in a ring will have a position in the ring, allowing a user to click sequentially from site to site all around the ring.

Wild Card. A symbol, such as an asterisk (*) or question mark (?) that substitutes in a search for any letter or set of letters of the alphabet (and sometimes for numerals, too). Thus, the expression *present** will match *present, presents, presented, presenter, presenting, presentation,* and so on. Sometimes, the asterisk is used to match one or more letters, while the question mark will match only one letter (with multiple question marks substituting for the same number of letters).

World Wide Web. The graphically based, global, hyperlinked collection of information sites on the Internet. The growth and popularity of the Web have made it the most popular part of the Internet. The Web's vast resources grow daily.

Net Notes

Use these pages to keep track of Web sites you find helpful or interesting.

4615